A Mountain Runner's Guide to Snowdonia

By
Jim Kelly

First published in Great Britain in 2010 by Trailguides Limited.
www.trailguides.co.uk

ISBN 978-1-905444-42-7

The route diagrams in this book are based upon 1925-1940 Ordnance Survey One Inch maps updated by field trips and site visits.

Trailguides Limited
35 Carmel Road South
Darlington
Co Durham DL3 8DQ

Cover design by Steve Gustard

CONTENTS

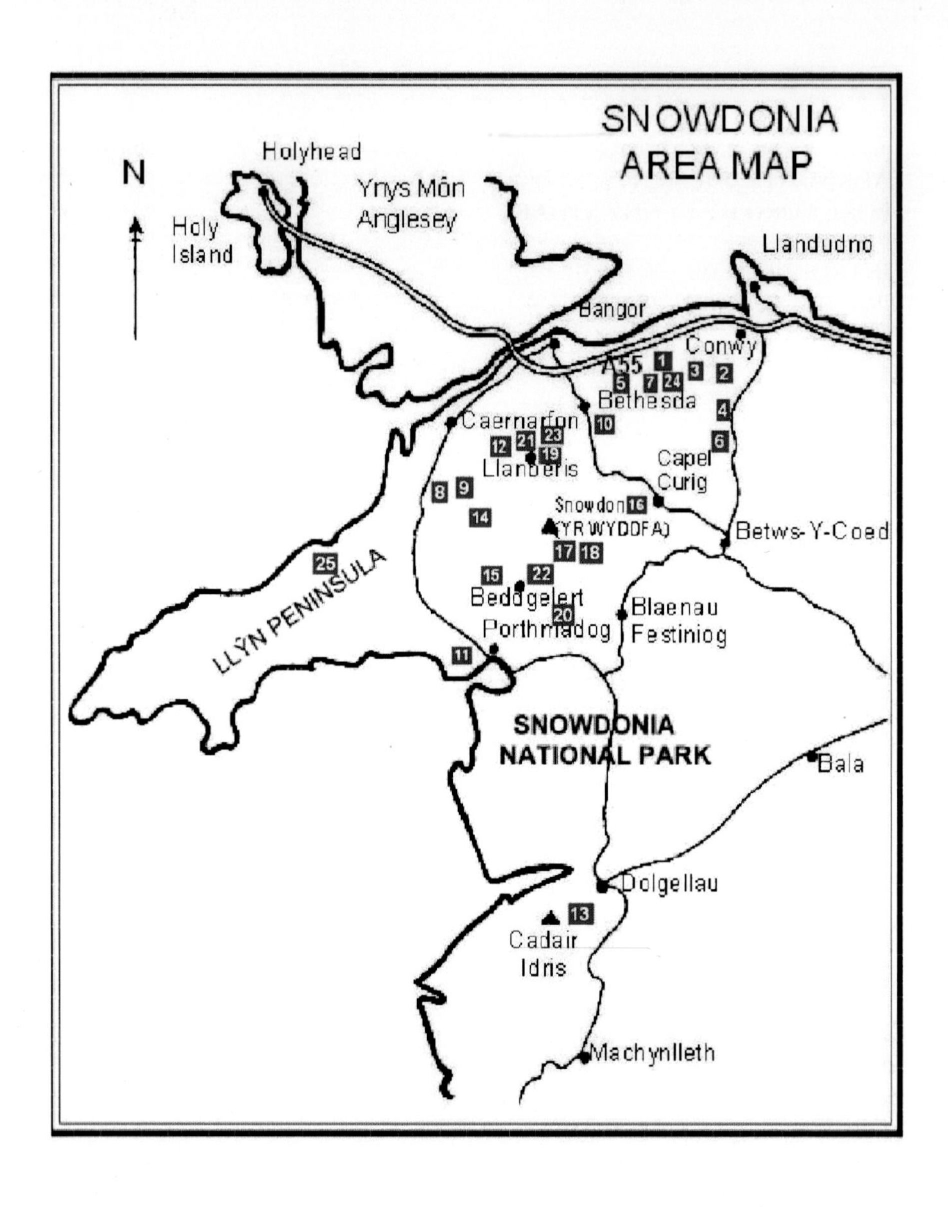
SNOWDONIA
AREA MAP
N
Holyhead
Holy
Island
Ynys Môn
Anglesey
Llandudno
Bangor
Conwy
A55
1
2
3
5
7
24
Bethesda
4
Caernarfon
10
12
21
23
19
6
Llanberis
Capel
Curig
8
9
Snowdon
16
14
(YR WYDDFA)
Betws-Y-Coed
17
18
25
LLŶN PENINSULA
15
22
Beddgelert
20
Blaenau
Festiniog
Porthmadog
11
SNOWDONIA
NATIONAL PARK
Bala
Dolgellau
13
Cadair
Idris
Machynlleth

ACKNOWLEDGEMENTS

The very existence of this new, definitive guide book to fell running in Snowdonia is owed to the dedicated efforts of a long list of friends and helpers. In particular I would like to thank the following:

I would like to thank the following: Phil Jones of Rhedwyr Eryri and Stephen Edwards of CREAD Design and Media for their route checking expertise and encouragement. The legendary mountain runner, Kenny Stuart, the current holder of the Snowdon Race record for 25 years(!), who very kindly accepted the offer to write the 'Foreword' to this guide. Also, members of the Eryri Committee who supported and encouraged me during the guides' production.

'Thank you' to Zac Laraman at Sports Resource.org for his invaluable advice surrounding running injury avoidance. It is something we all need to bear in mind when we are out on the hills either in training or competition.

Above all, I would like to thank my wife, Julia for hours of hand work either sat in-front of the laptop night after night producing text and graphics or, stood around on windswept hillsides snapping pictures of me! Her contribution to this guide has been enormous.

Final thanks go to Keven Shevels and Trailguides Ltd, for believing in me and giving this guide the 'green-light'.

Let us hope it will be the first of many.

Jim Kelly.

PARC CENEDLAETHOL ERYRI
SNOWDONIA
NATIONAL PARK

FOREWORD BY KENNY STUART

Reading this runner's guide brings back a myriad of memories of days spent racing and relaxing in Snowdonia. My wife and I always took the opportunity after competing in the Snowdon race and the Welsh 1000 metre peaks race to explore the paths and trails in the surrounding area and it would have been great to have had a guide such as this to make better use of the time available.

My three children have competed in various races in Snowdonia with both daughters contesting various GB trials on Snowdon and it has always been a pleasure to return. Trail running has tremendous potential for runners of all abilities, from the elite racer training for fell or road to the novice just out to enjoy the terrain and increase fitness and well being.

I would love to see more of these runners guides covering different areas of Britain including of course my beautiful Lake District.

Kenny Stuart
Snowdon Race record holder 1985

PREFACE

Snowdonia National Park, in North Wales, has long been the outdoor activity playground for both residents and visitors since way back in Victorian times. Its majestic, rugged mountains, rounded fells and dramatic coastlines have continually drawn interest from rock climbers, mountaineers, walkers, water-sports enthusiasts, cyclists and, of course, not forgetting, the thousands of ordinary, casual tourists that flock to the region year on year.

However, the largest activity "growth area" over the last few years has been the increase in numbers of men and women using the region for mountain and fell running. For sure, mountain running in Snowdonia has a historic and varied tradition and, indeed, some of the sports' greatest National fell runners established their reputations and records here. Back in the 1970's and 1980's, the likes of Paddy Buckley and Colin Donnelly were posting ground-breaking, personal best times on some of the areas longest challenges. Amazingly, many of these records hold and still remain unbroken, posing a considerable challenge for today's fell running "young guns" and elite runners. Of particular interest are the records established by Kenny Stuart and Robbie Bryson in 1985 during the famous (infamous?!) Snowdon Race. Although Robbie was first to the top in a staggering 39.47minutes, it was Kenny who pulled away on the descent and posted a record time of 1.02.29. Both records are still intact… 25 years on!!

So, why is mountain running becoming so popular? Well, apart from the obvious health-related benefits involved with the sport (see other TRAILGUIDES "Coaching Off-Road Running" Series publications), mountain running is also a very "accessible" pastime. It can be practised by almost any reasonably fit person with equipment a fraction of the cost of some other outdoor sports. Add to this a fantastic, diverse, scenic landscape, with stunning, challenging routes for all levels of ability, and one is left with what is perhaps the one of the most rewarding, enjoyable "running cocktails" to be consumed anywhere in the UK.

It is for these reasons I felt compelled to create this, all new, runner's guide to the area. Aimed at both the novice and experienced, the young or the veteran, whether resident or "out of county" visitor, this book will provide the mountain and fell runner with experienced, first-hand advice, detailed, accurate route descriptions, safety and environmental considerations and a wealth of other, invaluable local information that will serve to assist and enhance any runner's Snowdonia mountain and fell experience. With routes from easy-angled, 4 milers to demanding, "full-on" mountain challenges that form part of the Welsh Fell Running Association's race calendar, there is something here to suit everyone. And, for the "tickers" and "competitive upstarts" amongst us, there is even a tick-sheet thrown in for good measure!

Jim Kelly, 2010

TABLE 1

	TRAIL	FELL	MOUNTAIN
Description	Lowland and forest areas including urban, cultivated and forested locations.	Moorlands and upland areas which may include some upland cultivated and forestry areas plus possibly remote locations.	Upland and mountain areas including remote and isolated locations.
Height	Not usually above 1,000 feet but may go up to 2,500 feet	Usually above 1,000 feet, up to 2,500 feet and above.	Usually above 2,500 feet and up to 4,000 feet.
Way-marking	Usually	Limited	None
Terrain	Usually graded paths, tracks and trails but may include some off-trail	May include some graded paths, tracks and trails but mainly off-trail	Virtually all off-trail
Height gain	Limited height gain	May include considerable height gain	May include some severe height gain.
Effects of weather	Very limited effect	May be prone to sudden weather changes	Extreme weather a possibility
Navigational skills	None to basic	Basic to competent	Competent to expert
Equipment	Running - Trail shoes Possibly waterproofs Food and drink dependant upon route	Running - Trail/fell shoes Full waterproof cover. Possibly map and compass dependant upon route. Food and drink dependant upon route	Running - Fell shoes Full waterproof cover Map and compass Food and drink
Escape Routes	Yes	Some	Some to nil

TABLE 2

Score	**0**	**1**	**2**	**3**	**4**
Distance	Up to 6 miles	6 – 12 miles	12 – 18 miles	18 miles +	24 miles +
Navigation	No navigation skills needed	Basic navigation skills needed	Competent navigation skills needed	Expert navigation skills needed	
Terrain	75% + on graded track or path	50 – 75% on graded track or path 25 – 50% off track	25 -50% on graded track or path 50 – 75% off track	Under 25% on graded track or path Over 75% off track	
Remoteness	Urban	Countryside in fairly close proximity to habitation – at least 80% of the route within 2 miles	Countryside not in close proximity to habitation – less than 20% of the route within 2 miles	Remote, isolated location	
Height gain	Less than 100 ft per mile	Over 100 ft per mile	Over 125 ft per mile	Over 250 ft per mile	

Notes to Table 2

Graded paths = Well established paths with a stable surface.

Escape routes = The opportunity to cut the route short and return to the start without completing the full course in the event of weather changes or unforeseen incidents.

MAPS:

Three maps are required to cover the full area of Snowdonia National Park; Ordnance Survey 1:25,000 Explorer Maps **OL17** which covers the northern section, **OL18** the central and **OL23** the southern section. The relevant map will be shown in the details of the individual run. The hand drawn maps reproduced in this guide act as route diagrams only and do not contain the vital relief and other detailed information that the Ordnance Survey maps provide. Whilst under normal conditions they should be sufficient to guide you round the run they are not intended to replace the use of the relevant map. The hills and mountains of Snowdonia are wild and rough, which is part of their attraction, and the weather on these tops can be very changeable. It is quite possible to set off in brilliant sunshine and then to find that later, low cloud, mist and rain has come rolling in and visibility is very poor. The ability to navigate with map and compass is a required skill to safely run in these mountains and it would be extremely foolhardy to venture out with just this guide and no map. If you intend to purchase any or, all, of these maps may I suggest that you opt for the laminated version (s). Although more expensive, they are fully waterproof and will stand up to the rigors of being put in and out of hydration belts and packs far more than their ordinary paper counterparts. A non-laminated map in regular use in any mountain environment will last no time!

WEATHER:

The weather in Snowdonia can be very changeable even during the summer. The exposed altitude of some of these high mountains can make even a balmy summer's day seem cold and uninviting. When you are near the top of one of these high summits or plateaus, mist, wind and rain can be experienced no matter the time of year and this can change quite quickly catching the fell runner unaware. Indeed, many of the higher peaks, particularly in the Snowdon Group, can generate their own mini-weather systems. It is quite possible for the tops and rocky ridges to be shrouded in mist and drizzle while the surrounding valleys and coastal lowlands are bathed in glorious sunshine! The message is, don't misjudge this high country. Recent winters in Snowdonia have been quite harsh with snow lying on the highest peaks from as early as October through to early April!. Whether these climatic trends continue remains to be seen. Basically, no matter the time of year, when running in these mountains and fells, be prepared and equipped for all weather conditions.

Jim Kelly at the start of Dolgarrog "Pipe Dream". Photo by Julia Kelly.

EQUIPMENT:

This one is always tricky. What to wear? What not to wear? What to take with you? What to leave behind? What if I need this? What if I don't? As I have discovered during many training runs and events, it is very difficult to get it right every time. If you are new to the sport of mountain running may I suggest you also purchase a copy of "An Introduction to Trail and Fell Running" (Trailguides ISBN 978-1-905444-40-3) to accompany this area guide. There is a very good chapter on kit choice and mountain safety, especially if you are training alone! You will find, with experience and common sense, your ability to judge what you are likely to need will improve over time. A basic rule of thumb is, there is no point in packing enough kit to traverse the

Gobi Desert if your run is less than five or six miles across the lowlands in warm spring sunshine! However, if your journey is 12 miles plus, across high country in remote, unfamiliar mountains and likely to take 3 hours or more, with uncertain weather conditions, then it's a different story! Most importantly, travel light. Opt for wearing non-cotton based fabrics that resist moisture retention and wick away sweat. In spring and summer a lightweight vest, shorts and cap is fine. Also consider whether you may need sunbloc! However, in winter, a short or long-sleeved compression top, lightweight waterproof shell top and compression running tights "combo" might sound more sensible. It's a personal choice regarding whether to use either a hydration back-pack or waist belt, "bum-bag". Whichever one you feel more comfortable with, essential kit in both should include map (and this Trailguide?!), compass, whistle, watch/ GARMIN G.P.S., silver survival bag, energy drink/gel, **mobile phone(*)**, running hat/cap, gloves, "Buff" (optional) and wind/waterproof shell top/ bottoms. The most important thing is to be comfortable. Also, make sure that you pack a clean set of clothes and footwear in the car to get changed into afterwards. There's nothing worse than driving back to wherever(?) covered in mud, with soaking wet feet, wearing sweaty running kit, in a desperate battle to prevent the car windows from steaming up! Yep, we've all done it! Not pleasant. If you notice, choice of footwear has been omitted. In the past, fell and mountain running was dominated by Walsh Shoes. However, in the last few years, the choice has widened enormously with the likes of Montrail, Saloman and INOV8 producing specialist shoes for different terrain, events and foot-type. The advice is, if in doubt, seek specialist help from your running shop or club.

(*) ***Please note that although mobile network coverage across the UK is more or less complete – depending on your provider of course! However, please remember that signal strength in mountainous or hilly areas is unpredictable. Whilst it can be full strength on the summits, back down in the sheltered valleys, surrounded by cliffs, it often fluctuates between one or two bars or, at worse, no signal whatsoever. The advice is; by all means take a mobile but be mindful that it could fail when you need it most! (see section on Mountain Safety/Emergency Procedures)***

INJURY AVOIDANCE :

Mountain running like any other form of physical activity places stresses and strains upon your musculoskeletal system so it's of the utmost importance that your system is in good health and repair to deal with these stresses. A good warm up routine and daily stretching is required to balance the exertions you place upon your body, without this you are likely to accumulate strains which may eventually turn into a long term injury and prevent you from doing what you love to do. This is rather important for mountain running, where the stresses and strains are magnified due to the uneven terrain, steep ascents and descents. In 'normal' running the forces through each footstep are equivalent to between 9 and 13 times your bodyweight, these forces need to be transmitted and dissipated through your healthy joints and flexible muscles. When you venture into the mountains these forces may be increased!! If you know you have an injury or feel a twinge you NEED to get it checked out by a suitable medical professional......DON'T HOPE FOR THE BEST!! Mountain rescue will not be impressed and a helicopter ride isn't what you set out for in the first place! Make sure you are adequately hydrated, fit and healthy and that your body is more than able to cope with the stresses of mountain running.

MOUNTAIN SAFETY AND EMERGENCY PROCEDURES:

Safety has got to be on the mind of every runner whether you are just running round the block or running in the high mountains of Snowdonia. The safety of yourself and anybody that you are running with, first of all rests with yourself. Even on a relatively "safe" low level route accidents and injuries can and do happen. If you are running alone, always tell someone where you are going and when you expect to be back. However, don't forget to tell them that you **are** back. Otherwise, you run the risk of causing, what Mountain Rescue define as, a "false call with good intent!"

If a serious accident does occur that requires you to be immobile then stop and try to find some shelter. If you are carrying a survival bag/space blanket use it. Ensure that you maintain your body temperature. Having stopped running you will quickly get chilled and cold. Use your whistle or mobile phone to summon help. The International Distress Call is six strong blasts of the whistle followed by a minutes silence, then repeat as necessary. Also, remember the point already mentioned regarding mobile phone signal limitations. However, if your phone has signal, **dial 999 and ask for North Wales Police, Mountain Safety.** If you manage to get through, the **MRT** (Mountain Rescue Team) will require essential factual information such as your location, grid reference (if possible), person involved and extent of the injury.

In the event of a helicopter evacuation, **ALL** runners or persons in the immediate area should take heed; A helicopter flying close to rocks or ridges will make verbal communication between anyone on the ground almost impossible. Be wary of any loose debris being blown around by the rotor downdraft. An orange smoke grenade may be dropped from the helicopter to give wind direction. Assistance should only be given to the helicopter crew/ personnel if requested. A helicopter will always be flown into the wind to effect a rescue and, on landing, there are three danger points; the main rotor, the tail rotor and the engine exhaust. The helicopter should not be approached until directed to do so by the air crew.

Remember, you can reduce the risk to yourself and others by ensuring that you plan and time your runs effectively, carry and wear the correct equipment, possess adequate navigational knowledge/skills and pay attention to local weather conditions. If in doubt, be prepared to adapt/modify your run accordingly. Occasionally, it is wise to allow discretion to be the better part of running valour!

WHERE TO STAY:

Like in any of the UK's National Park designated areas, the list of places to stay in Snowdonia is probably about as long as the rail tracks extending from

Llanberis to Snowdon summit! However, as a starting point, I have listed several establishments that offer a warm welcome and reasonable rates for an overnight stay or two.

Camping/ Bunkhouse Accommodation:

Pentre Bach (Bach Ventures Ltd.) Campsite & Bunkhouse, Waunfawr, Nr. Caernarfon LL54 7AG. Nice campsite, great location, barn sleeps up to 16 persons. Tel: 01286 650643.

Pete's Eats, 40 High Street, Llanberis LL55 4EU. Bunkhouse/ dormitory accommodation. Tel: 01286 870117. Website: www.petes-eats.co.uk

Eric's Café, Campsite & Bunkhouse, Bwlch y Moch, Tremadog, Gwynedd LL49 9SN. Owned by Eric Jones, the legendary climber, mountaineer, free-fall parachutist and 'original' adrenaline junkie! Amazingly, he's still doing it all and he's in his seventies! Great location for southern/ central Snowdonia runs. Tel: 01766 512199/ 0777 1482321 for bookings. Email: climbtremadog@aol.com

Tyddyn Llwyn Caravan & Touring Park, Morfa Bychan Road, Porthmadog, Gwynedd LL49 9UR. Situated beneath Moel y Gest, this is an ideal location for runners owning a caravan/camper van. Very sheltered site and the owner, Peter Wright, is very 'pro-fell running". Tent pitches also available. Tel: 01766 512205. Website: www.tyddynllwyn.com

Hotels/ Bed & Breakfast:

Lakeview Hotel, Tan-y-Pant, Llanberis LL55 4EL.
Proprietor Michael and Carrie Sims. Welcoming, privately owned hotel overlooking Llyn Padarn. Popular restaurant offering varied menu with local produce, also gluten and dairy free choices (including beers and lagers).
Tel: 01286 870422. Website : www.lakeviewhotel.co.uk

The Legacy Royal Victoria Hotel, Llanberis LL55 4TY. The 'original' hotel in Llanberis. Big and 'touristy' but that's part of its charm. Tel: 0870 832 9903. Website : www.legacy-hotels.co.uk

Gallt-y-Glyn Hotel, Llanberis, Gwynedd, LL55 4EL. Small, private hotel, function room also available. Great home-made,"Create your own Pizza and a Pint" menu! This place gets busy so ring to book a table, especially on Fridays and Saturdays. Very popular with climbers. Russ & Heidi will welcome you with great food and log fires! Tel. 01286 870370. Website : www.gallt-y-glyn.co.uk

WHERE TO EAT:

Being the tourist destination it is, Snowdonia has a massive variety of restaurants, cafes, pubs and takeaways. Like anywhere, some are exceptionally good, some are bad and some are.. well, downright ugly! Depending on your location/ 'base-camp', you may wish to consider any of the following;

Pete's Eats, 38-40 High Street, Llanberis. Pete's is an 'institution' and has been the 'focal-point'/ meeting place for rock climbers, walkers, cyclists etc. for as long as anyone can remember. Offers great food and lots of it at reasonable prices. The menu should satisfy any runner's appetite at the end of a tough day out on the fells. Open 8am – 8pm. Website : www.petes-eats.co.uk

Asha Balti House, Denbigh Street, Llanwrst, Nr. Conwy LL26 0LL.Tel: 01492 641910 (www.asha-balti-house.co.uk). Award winning curry house. Probably

the best in North Wales! Excellent menu, service and atmosphere.

Gallt-y-Glyn Hotel, Caernarfon Road, Llanberis, LL55 4EL. Tel: 01286 870370. Great home-made, "Create your own Pizza and a Pint" menu! This place gets busy so ring to book a table, especially on Fridays and Saturdays. Very popular with climbers.

Le Bistro, 23 Hole in the Wall Street, Caernarfon LL55 1RF. Tel. 01286 672131. e-mail lebistro23@aol.com. Owned by Jacky and Linda Boulet. Jacky is a very active fell runner so a warm welcome is guaranteed to anyone producing or mentioning this book when they order! "Tres bon cuisine!"

Pen y Ceunant Isaf Tea Rooms,
Snowdon Path, Llanberis LL55 4UW. Tel: 01286 872606. Restored 18th C. Cottage cafe en route to Snowdon summit. Log fire, tea, cakes and locally bottled real ales. Fantastic!

TOURIST INFORMATION CENTRES & WEBSITES:

Within Snowdonia there are... wait for it, 11 (yes, 11!) Tourist Information Centres (TIC's) serving the mountains and coastal regions. There are also 6 "Snowdonia National Park Information Centres". Contact details for the main TIC's are as follows:

Llanberis Tourist Information Centre, 41A High Street, Llanberis. Tel: 01286 870765.

Beddgelert Tourist Information Centre, Canolfan Hotel Hebog, Beddgelert. Tel: 01766 890615.

Dolgellau Tourist Information Centre, Ty Meirion, Eldon Square, Dolgellau. Tel:01341 422888.

Snowdonia Nat. Park Information Centre (Betws-y-Coed). Tel: 01690 710426.

Snowdonia Nat. Park Information Centre (Blaenau Ffestiniog). Tel: 01766 830360.

In addition to the TIC's the Snowdonia National Park Authority also operate a very useful website giving information on places to visit, places to eat and shop as well as advice on other leisure activities in the area. The website can be found at: www.eryri-npa.gov.uk

Other websites worth looking are: www.attractionsofsnowdonia.com and www.visitsnowdonia.info

FELL RUNNING WEBSITES:

For specific information relating to Snowdonia/ Welsh fell running, races and results contact:

Rhedwyr ERYRI Harriers Running Club: www.eryriharriers.org.uk

Welsh Fell Runners Association (WFRA): www.wrfa.org.uk

Welsh Athletics (Athletau Cymru) Ltd: www.welshathletics.org

Appendix 1:

"The Paddy Buckley Round"

Although not mentioned in this guide as a specific route, this historic run is synonymous with North Wales Ultra running. This famous challenge begins at Llanberis and takes in the Glyders and, Ogwen, then on to Capel Curig via the Carneddau Range, and down to Aberglaslyn and the Moelwyns. It then veers back up to Rhyd Ddu via Hebog and the Nantlle Ridge, with a final assault on Snowdon and Moel Eilio, leading back into Llanberis. Indeed, some of the elements of this run are included in this guide as individual routes... it is linking them together that forms the whole route! Completion time is normally within a 24 hour period but this is so dependent on many factors i.e., weather, ground conditions and individual fitness etc. It is for these reasons it is not included in the main narrative of this guide. Due to its distance and logistical planning, it is not a run where you simply park up, exit your car, run and return in a few hours and then drive home! Quite the contrary. It requires a very high level in terms of fitness, planning and logistical organisation and backup.

However, it is a highly respected route challenge. Much information can be found online by keying in ***"Paddy Buckley Round"*** into any good search engine box. Alternatively, a full description of the route and its various stages can be found by obtaining a copy of *"The Welsh Three Thousand Foot Challenges"* by Ed Clayton and Ron Turnbull.

ABER FALLS & NORTH WALES PATH CIRCUIT
ROUTE 1

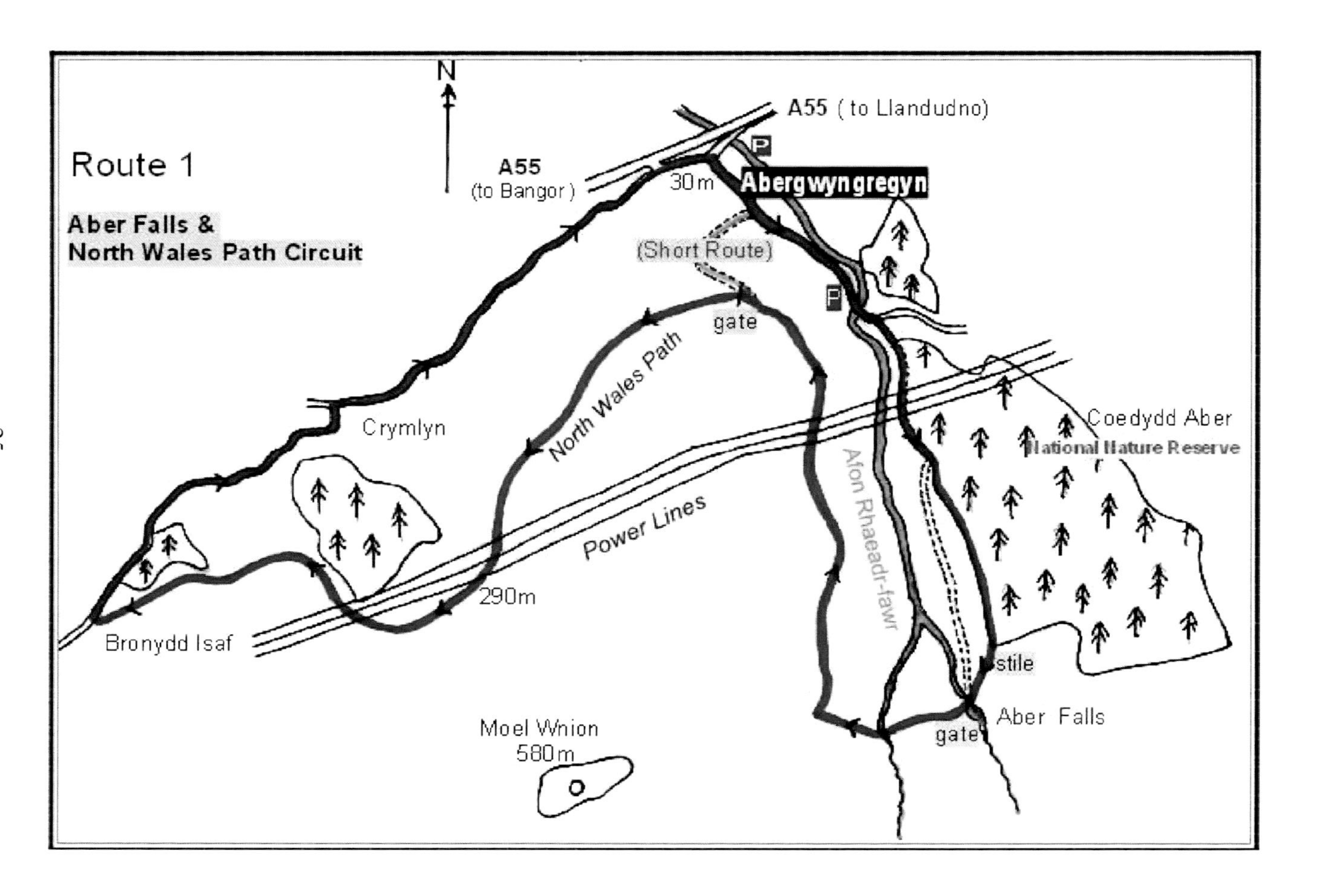
Route 1
Aber Falls &
North Wales Path Circuit
N
A55
(to Bangor)
A55 (to Llandudno)
P
Abergwyngregyn
30m
(Short Route)
P
gate
North Wales Path
Crymlyn
Power Lines
290m
Bronydd Isaf
Afon Rhaeadr-fawr
Coedydd Aber
National Nature Reserve
stile
Aber Falls
gate
Moel Wnion
580m

ROUTE 1: ABERFALLS & NORTH WALES PATH CIRCUIT

DISTANCE: 8 Miles
ASCENT: Min. 30metres @ start. Max. 290metres.
TERRAIN: A route of considerable character which includes the famous 150' high "Aber Falls". A good valley run with fantastic coastal views towards the Menai Strait and Isle of Anglesey in its latter stages. No real hazards and reasonably sheltered from the elements owing to its valley location. An ideal lower-level alternative route when the nearby Carneddau mountains are experiencing inclement weather conditions. Defined valley and hillside footpaths and tarmac lane. Occasional rocks and tree roots.
TIME: 1 Hour 20 mins. Approx.
START: Abergwngregyn Village
O.S MAP: 1:25,000 Sheet North Wales OL17.
GRADIENT: Gentle
ACCESS: Park in the village of Abergwyngregyn (G.R.654727), just off A55 coast road just after or before Llanfairfechan. Cars can be parked, free of charge, a little way up from the village bus stop/ turn-around spot. Please try to avoid parking in the village itself. The roads are narrow and spaces very limited.

Grid References

654727	Parking area in Abergwyngregyn
668701	Track through pine forest
668701	The famous Aber Falls waterfall
661675	Cart track
657721	North Wales Footpath
627705	Bronydd Isaf
639715	Crymlyn

FGS Grading: Grading is F4 [D1, N1,T0,R1,H1]

Distance	**1**	6 – 12 miles
Navigation	**1**	Basic navigation skills needed
Terrain	**0**	75% + on graded track or path
Remoteness	**1**	Countryside in fairly close proximity to habitation – at least 80% of the route within 2 miles
Height	**1**	Over 100ft. per mile.

Exposed tree roots can pose a hazard on this run.
Photo by Julia Kelly.

Route Description :

1. Run from the car park through the village passing the cafe, 'Hen Felin', after a few hundred yards. Remember this spot on your return… nice coffee and even nicer cakes ☺ … Continue gently uphill to the Aber Falls pay & display car park. Bear left over the bridge crossing the Afon Rhaedr Fawr and turn immediately right passing the large 'Aber' forestry commission sign.

2. Now run the gently ascending gravel track for approximately half a mile to where a path branches left through the pine trees (no pun intended!).Take this **(GR.665713)** as it rises delightfully between the Larch trees, taking care with the occasional exposed roots. Eventually, a stile is reached which leads onto the open, scree-covered hillside. Directly ahead one can see (and hear!) the famous Aber Falls

Emerging from the trees before reaching Aber Falls. Photo by Julia Kelly.

(**GR.668701**). A tourist attraction since Victorian times, this huge plume of water drains the catchment area known as Cwm yr Afon Goch. This is particularly impressive after heavy rain as it cascades over 150' into its water-carved plunge pool.

3. From the falls cross over the wooden footbridge and up the other side passing through a gate sign posted 'North Wales Path'. Run the rocky path in a westerly direction passing over another small wooden footbridge with the steep eastern slopes of Moel Wnion (580m) ahead of you. However, from here, the route swings rightwards and upwards in a northerly direction, eventually connecting with a gently rising cart track (**GR.661675**) which roughly follows the 260m contour line. Run this, passing under the impressive electricity pylons that span the valley. Continue to **GR.657721** where the North Wales Path continues in a west, south westerly direction. It is worth mentioning here that it is possible to take a rightward descending cart track that meets another path after approx. quarter of a mile. Run down the narrow, steep, right branch and return to Aber village, emerging only a couple of hundred yards up from the café. This reduces the run to 4.5 miles.

4. Returning to the North Wales Path, run the near horizontal, defined track with a slight rise to the 290m contour, the route's highest point, as it passes, once again, under the power lines. The path now gently descends through farmland until it joins a single-track tarmac lane marked "Bronydd Isaf" on the OS Map (**GR. 627705**). Turn right here and run the pleasant twisting lane via Crymlyn (**GR. 639715**) back to Abergwygregyn.

FOEL LŴS
ROUTE 2

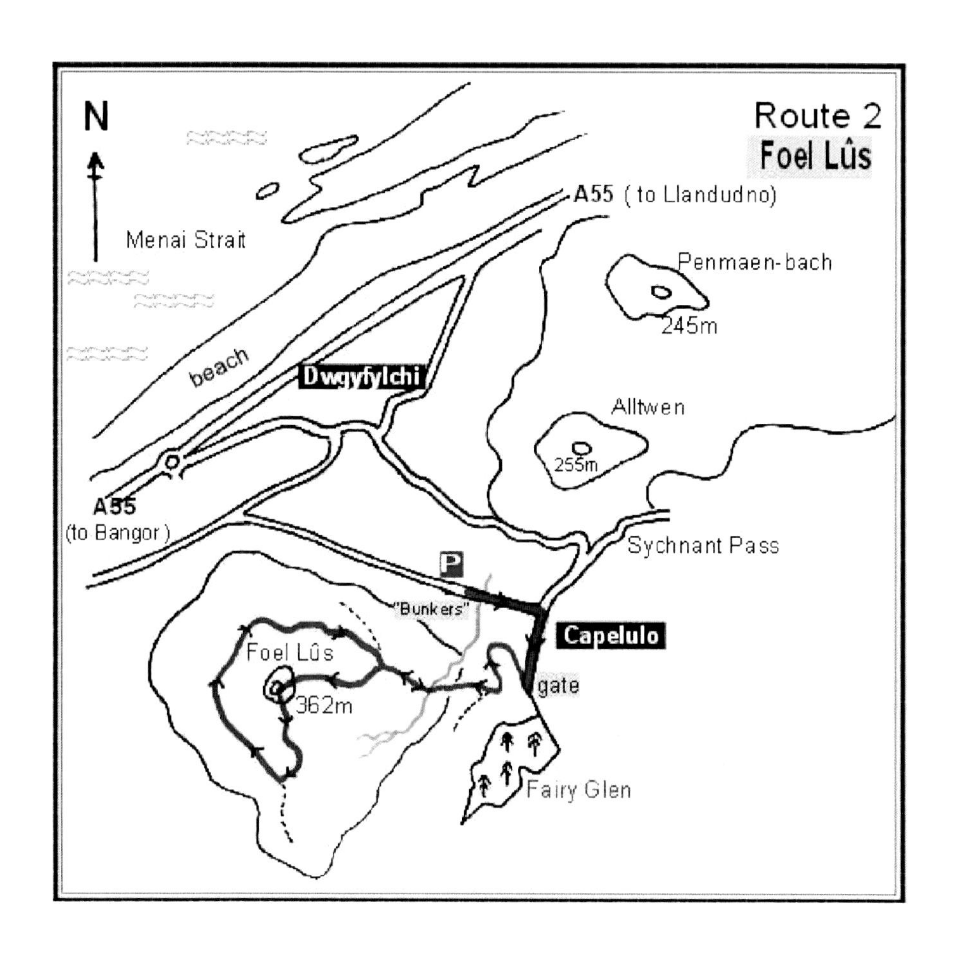
N
Route 2
Foel Lûs
A55 (to Llandudno)
Menai Strait
Penmaen-bach
245m
beach
Dwgyfylchi
Alltwen
255m
A55
(to Bangor)
Sychnant Pass
P
"Bunkers"
Capelulo
Foel Lûs
gate
362m
Fairy Glen

ROUTE 2: FOEL LÛS

DISTANCE: 3.3 Miles
ASCENT: Min. 69 metres @ start. Max. 362 metres.
TERRAIN: Although a relatively short route, uphill interest is maintained all the way to the summit. Delightful downhill section with fast, flat cart track in the latter half of the route. Stunning sea views of the North Wales coast line and Menai Strait. Defined hill footpaths and stony cart track.
TIME: 30 – 40 minutes depending on ability.
START: Capelulo Village
O.S MAP: 1:25,000 Sheet North Wales OL17.
GRADIENT: Continually rising, steep in places. Level 'coach road' section.
ACCESS: Locate "Bunker's" Golf Bar/ Restaurant. Park cars here in a lay-by opposite.

Grid References

743766	Parking lay-by
739763	Small stream crossing
733757	Junction of path with Coach Road.

FGS Grading: Grading is F4 [D0, N0,T0,R1,H3]

Distance	**0**	Up to 6 miles.
Navigation	**0**	No navigation skills needed.
Terrain	**0**	75% + on graded track or path.
Remoteness	**1**	Countryside in fairly close proximity to habitation – at least 80% of route within 2 miles.
Height	**3**	Over 250 ft per mile.

Route Description :

1. Run towards the village of Capelulo taking the lane forking rightwards between two public houses; "The Fairy Glen" and "The Dwygyfylchi". This gradually rises for approximately ¼ mile until it reaches a sharp turn right up an often muddy farm track (gate - plcase close this after you). Continue along this as it swings round leftwards. At approximately the 200m contour one leaves this broad track and follows a narrower, less-defined route upwards, negotiating a small stream at **GR.739763**. A short boggy section follows that becomes drier as the path rises steeply once again. Continue to where a flat, cart track is reached by a telegraph pole (remember this for your return!). Follow the cart track for a few metres in a northerly direction locating a narrow path on your left ascending through heather and rocks. Remain on this as it wends its way to the summit cairn at 362 metres.

Runners during the 2010 annual Foel Lus fell race. Photo by Julia Kelly

2. On reaching the top, immediately descend the narrow, stony path in a Southerly direction swinging round to the west in its lower part. (Don't make the mistake of forking left here.) Now descend a short bank onto the good, flat "coach road" (**GR.733757**) that circumnavigates the whole mountain. Your landmark here is 2 high stone pillars at the star of the coach road. Cars are sometimes parked here.

3. Now run this fast, horizontal track around the mountain. On a clear day, the views across Menai Strait and Anglesey are magnificent. Very soon (depending on your speed!) you will reach the aforementioned telegraph pole. From here, your descent is the exact reverse at the ascent, only faster! An average time for this run would be around 30 - 40 minutes.

PENMAENMAWR 3 HILLS
ROUTE 3

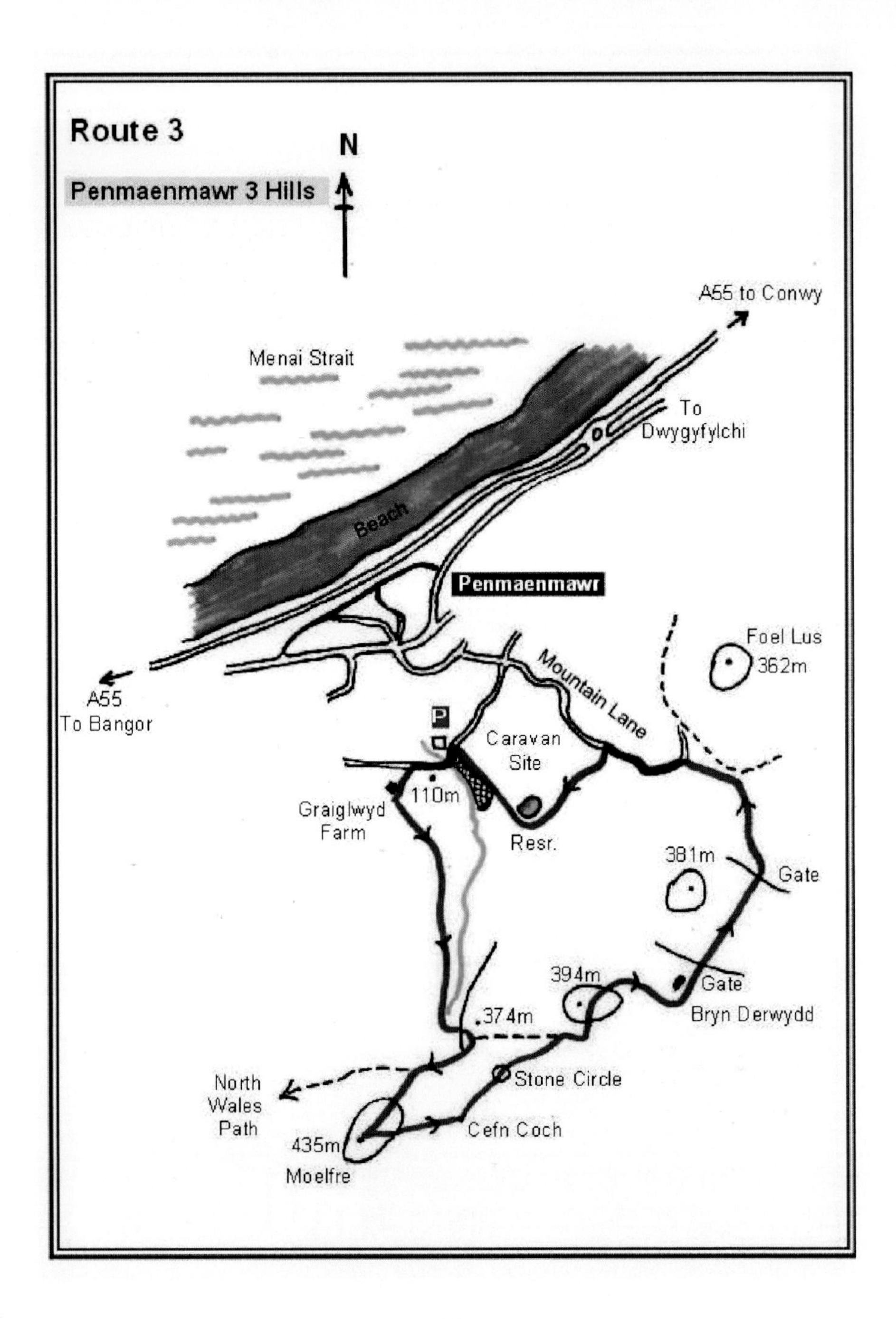
Route 3
N
Penmaenmawr 3 Hills
A55 to Conwy
Menai Strait
To
Dwygyfylchi
Beach
Penmaenmawr
A55
To Bangor
Mountain Lane
Foel Lus
362m
P
Caravan
Site
110m
Graiglwyd
Farm
Resr.
381m
Gate
394m
Gate
Bryn Derwydd
374m
Stone Circle
North
Wales
Path
Cefn Coch
435m
Moelfre

ROUTE 3: PENMAENMAWR 3 HILLS

DISTANCE: 3.5 Miles
ASCENT: Min. 100 metres @ start. Max. 435 metres.
TERRAIN: A route of similar terrain to neighbouring Foel Lûs and Tal-y-Fan and a variation to an annual Tuesday Night Fell Race. In addition to this, the whole area is significant in terms of its history, dating back to the Bronze Age and the Druids. Much of this evidence is visible during this run.
Although not especially high in terms of difficulty, please note, this area can experience sudden changes in weather owing to its close proximity to the coast and the Carneddau Range of mountains to the south. Sea mist can rise very quickly and envelop the tops of these hills very rapidly. Bear this factor in mind if considering any 'innovative' loops or any extensions to this route. In particular, with regard to navigation and route-finding issues.
As with all routes, it is prudent to check the local weather forecast beforehand. The majority of the terrain is on good paths or tracks with some 'wetness' in one or two spots!
TIME: 40 – 55 minutes (longer if looking at stone circles!)
START: Parking area opposite Craiglwyd Hall Caravan Park, Penmaenmawr.
O.S MAP: 1:25,000 Sheet North Wales OL17.
GRADIENT: Initial long steady ascent. Downhill and flat sections thereafter.
ACCESS: No known access issues.

Grid References

722759	Parking area opposite Craiglwyd Hall Caravan Site.
721748	Concrete footbridge.
718746	Moelfre 435m.
722745	Stone cairn (Cefn Coch).
723746	'Druids Stone Circle'.
730749	Bryn Derwydd.
733757	Footpath forks left.
725757	Reservoir/ fishing lake.

FGS Grading: Grading is: F6 [D0, N1, T1, R1, H3)

Distance	0	Up to 6 miles.
Navigation	1	Basic navigation skills needed.
Terrain	1	50 – 75% on graded track or path. 25 – 50% off track.
Remoteness	1	Countryside in fairly close proximity to habitation – at least 80% of the route within 2 miles.
Height	3	Over 250 ft per mile.

The Author, Jim Kelly descending from Cefn Coch towards the Druids Stone Circle. Photo by Julia Kelly.

Route Description :

1. This "sister" route to Foel Lûs (Route 2), includes the series of low hills to the south west of it. The route begins at the upper part of the village of Penmaenmawr at **GR 722759**. Park in the small area of land opposite 'Craiglwyd Hall Caravan Site'. From here, run up the country lane taking the first left turn up towards Craiglwyd Farm. A signposted public footpath takes you past the farmhouse and onto open country, via a metal kissing gate.

2. A grassy path rises continually, crossing over a concrete footbridge, constructed to avoid a wet, marshy area (**GR 721748**). Follow the path to another metal kissing gate in a wall and turn right. After a very short distance the North Wales Path is met. Run a little way along this in a westerly direction until a vague path on the left can be followed through heather and bilberry to the rounded top of Moelfre (435m) **GR 718746**, the highest point on this route.

3. From Moelfre, descend easterly towards a pile of stones at Cefn Coc (**GR 722745**). Descend a worn grassy track towards the "Druids Stone Circle" (interesting place and worth a quick look!!) at **GR 723746**.

4. Continue your descent to the North Wales Path once again. Cross this and run uphill to point '394m.' marked as 'Ffridd Wanc' on the OS Map. Drop down off this by running easterly to end up at the metal gate leading to Bryn Derwydd (**GR 730749**). A good coach road/ farm track is now followed towards Foel Lûs.

5. At **GR 733757**, the path forks. Take the left fork steeply downwards towards the minor road, known as 'Mountain Lane', leading back in to Penmaenmawr Village.

The steep descent towards Mountain Lane. Photo by Julia Kelly.

6. On reaching the lane, turn left and follow it downwards until a signed public footpath on the left takes ones across fields towards the 'reservoir' at **GR 725757**. Go through a metal gate and run past the fishing lake and caravan site. The track you are now on emerges directly opposite your vehicle. How convenient!

For those wishing to extend this route there are a number of options: The logical link is to combine this route with an ascent of Foel Lûs (see Route 2) or, for the more adventurous, across the moorlands stretching towards Tal-y-Fan (see Route 4) and the surrounding area. A large network of paths exist in this area so there is a huge choice. **However, please note, the navigation skills would require an up-grading to FGS 2 if any extensions were made to this route.**

TAL-Y-FAN
ROUTE 4

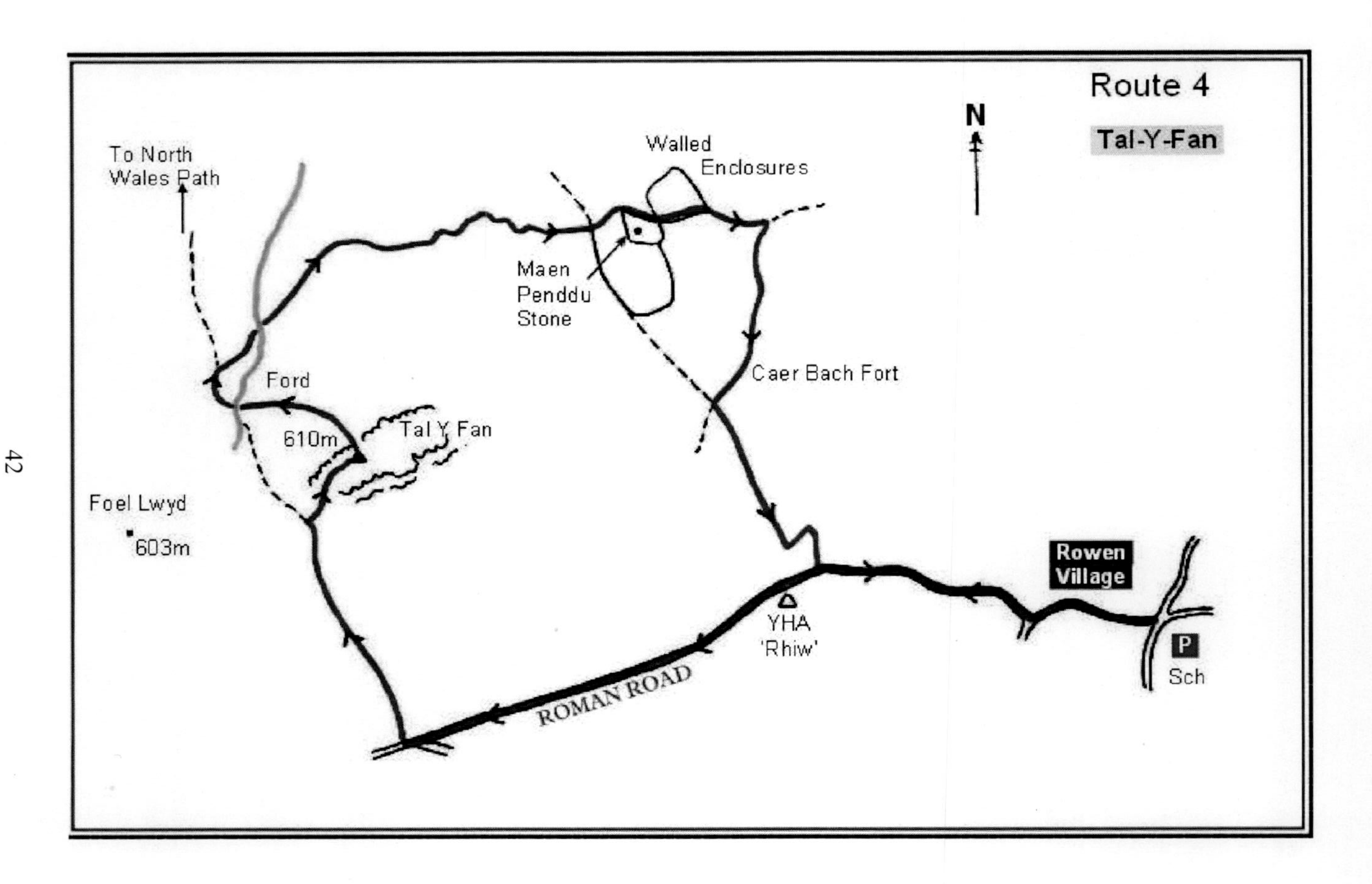

Route 4
Tal-Y-Fan
N
To North Wales Path
Walled Enclosures
Maen Penddu Stone
Caer Bach Fort
Ford
610m
Tal Y Fan
Foel Lwyd
603m
Rowen Village
YHA 'Rhiw'
P
Sch
ROMAN ROAD

ROUTE 4: TAL-Y-FAN

DISTANCE: 8.7 Miles
ASCENT: Min.50 metres @ start. Max.610 metres.
TERRAIN: At 610m, Tal y Fan is the smallest of the Snowdonia 'mountains'. The area is also considerably rich in prehistoric settlements and Roman remains. The OS Map shows these quite clearly. From a runner's perspective, the area is perfect, comprising of open moor lands, steep slopes, well-defined paths and tracks and great views. The large 'network' of high country paths means that a run, such as this, can be extended very easily with little height gained or lost. The route described here follows the annual fell race route held each year at the Rowen Village Summer Carnival, usually held in July.
TIME: 1hr 30 – 40 minutes.
START: Rowen Village, Nr. Conwy GR 758719. Park just before the village just after the school.
O.S MAP: 1:25,000 Sheet North Wales OL17.
GRADIENT: Several steep sections en route to the top of Tal y Fan, both on and off-road.
ACCESS: No access issues.

Grid References

758719	Rowen Village.
747721	Youth Hostel marked as 'Rhiw'.
732715	Junction between Roman Road track and tarmac minor road.
729726	Summit of Tal y Fan @ 610m.
725728	Stream crossing point (ford)/ defined path.
741735	'Maen Penddu Standing Stone'
746735	Wide Track
744730	'Caer Bach Fort'
748722	Steep lane leading back to Rowen

FGS Grading: Grading is F9 [D1, N2, T1,R2,H3]

Distance	**1**	6 – 12 miles
Navigation	**2**	Competent navigation skills needed.
Terrain	**1**	50 – 75% on graded track or path 25 – 50% off track.
Remoteness	**2**	Countryside not in close proximity to habitation – less than 20% of the route within 2 miles.
Height	**3**	Over 250 ft per mile.

Following the grassy track up towards the summit of Tal Y Fan.
Photo by Julia Kelly.

Route Description :

1. From Rowen run along the village road past the pub on the right. Where the road splits, choose the right hand fork as it climbs uphill – steep in parts, especially near the top as one approaches the Y.H.A. building, marked as 'Rhiw' on the OS map (**GR 747721**). The road now 'dissolves' and flattens out somewhat into a rough cart track which is the remains of a Roman Road. Running with 'Gladiatorial determination', remain on this until another tarmac road is met at GR 732715. Immediately after this, a ladder stile in the wall on the right. This allows access to open country and a grassy footpath (boggy in places), which leads steadily upwards across the moor land in the direction of Tal y Fan, passing over several more stiles. The top of Tal y Fan is reached by taking a less-defined, rocky path to the summit trig point at 610 m. (**GR 729726**).

Following the grassy track up towards the summit of Tal Y Fan.
Photo by Julia Kelly.

2. From here descend steeply in a north westerly direction over heather, grassy tussocks and boggy ground until the defined footpath is met once again at **GR 725728**. 'Ford' the small stream and continue along this path as it swings round in an easterly direction towards an area marked on the map as 'Maen Penddu Standing Stone' (**GR 741735**). Here, several footpaths converge.

3. Keeping the standing stone on your right, run between two areas of walled enclosure emerging, after a short distance, at a wide track (**GR 746735**). Turn right here onto the track and run in a southerly direction as it passes the site of 'Caer Bach Fort' (**GR 744730**). Just after this, another path crosses. Turn left and descend the grassy hillside towards the Y.H.A. building. Another path is met before the Y.H.A. which allows one to emerge at the top of the steep lane leading back to Rowen (**GR 748722**). A fast descent down the tarmac into the village is all that remains.

MOEL-Y-CI
ROUTE 5

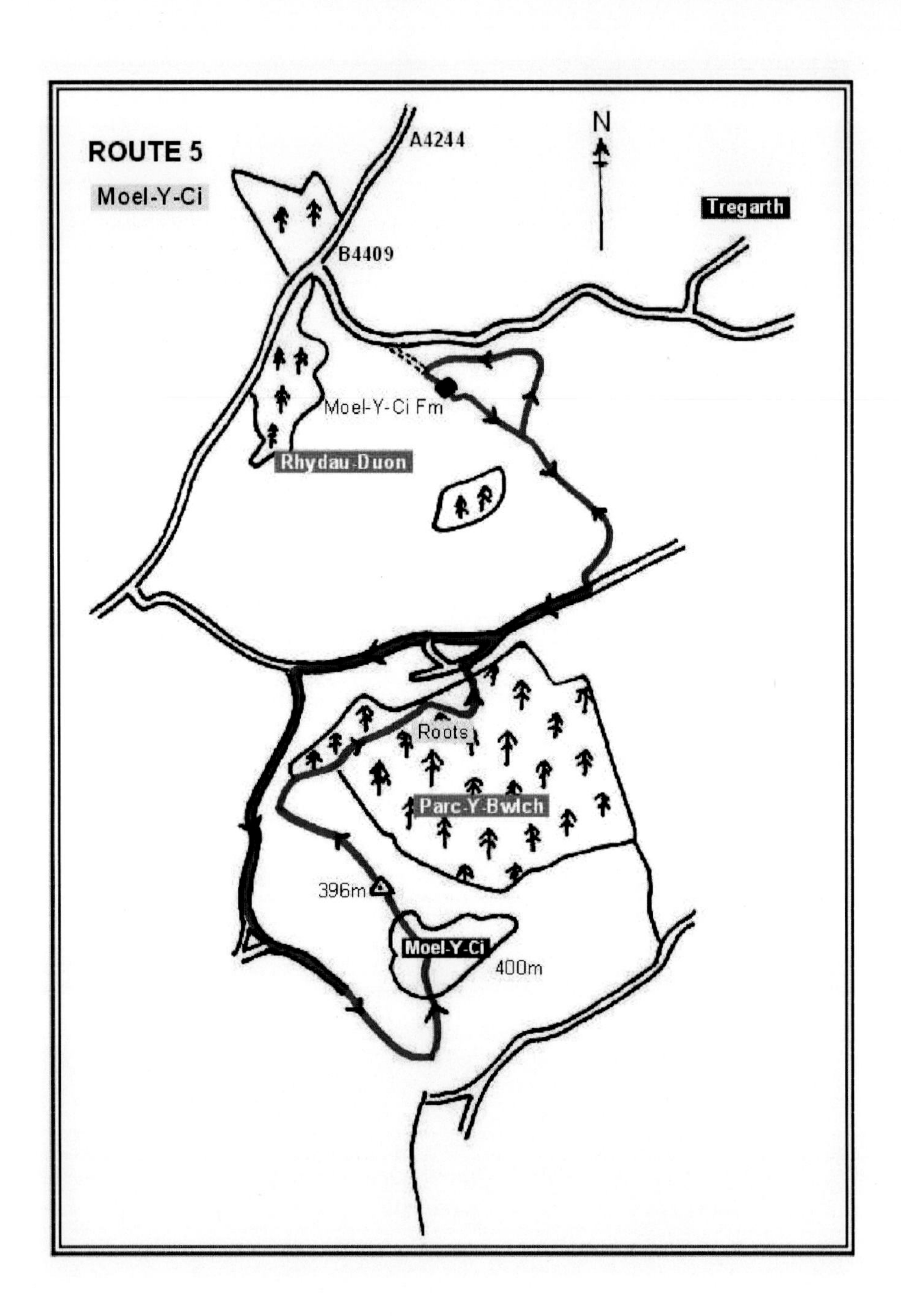
ROUTE 5
Moel-Y-Ci
A4244
N
Tregarth
B4409
Moel-Y-Ci Fm
Rhydau-Duon
Roots
Parc-Y-Bwlch
396m
Moel-Y-Ci
400m

ROUTE 5: MOEL Y CI

DISTANCE: 5 Miles
ASCENT: Min.110 metres @ start. Max.400 metres.
TERRAIN: A varied mix of farmland, tracks, hill slopes and woodland trails. Although a relatively short route, a determined approach is needed in order to run a good time. This is a popular fell race each year in the ERYRI/ WFRA's calendar in February. Always well-attended.
TIME: Anywhere between 40mins and 1hr 10 depending on ability.
START: Moel y Ci Farm/ Environmental Centre.
O.S MAP: 1:25,000 Sheet North Wales OL17.
GRADIENT: Steady, steep in places.
ACCESS: From the A55 coast road, exit at junction 12 towards Bethesda. At the small roundabout take the A4244 to Llanberis. Continue for just over a mile. Turn left on to the B4409 towards Tregarth. After a few hundred metres one sees the huge slate sign of 'Moel y Ci' farm on the right. Park on the verge side a little way on from this. No access issues but bear in mind Moel y Ci Farm is a dwelling. Do not obstruct the farm's driveway, do not drop litter and do not use the land as a 'toilet!'

Grid References

594678	Moel y Ci Farm (starting point)
599673	Wall
587668	Road junction
642655	Wall and gate
586664	Path intersection with rough track
593667	Sharp turn in woods
596676	Change of direction onto vague path

FGS Grading: Grading is F4 [D0, N1, T1,R1,H1]

Distance	**0**	5 miles
Navigation	**1**	Basic navigation skills needed
Terrain	**1**	50-75% on graded track or path. 25-50% off track.
Remoteness	**1**	Countryside in fairly close proximity to habitation- at least 80% of the route within 2 miles.
Height	**1**	Over 100ft per mile.

Steve Jones about to finish in the 2010 Moel Y Ci fell race.
Photo Julia Kelly.

Route Description :

1. Begin this run by entering the gravel driveway leading up to Moel y Ci Farm / Environmental Centre (**G.R.594678**). Follow the defined, gently rising track through the farm and proceed in a south easterly direction through some pasture land. At **G.R.599673** thc path swings around to the right following a dry stone wall until a stile is reached which provides access to a tarmac lane. Continue for a short distance along this until a path is met descending gently downhill to another tarmac lane. Follow this to a road junction at **G.R.587668**. Turn sharp left here and run steeply uphill. At 'Rallt Uchaf' this road becomes a rough track that contours and gently rises around the hill of Moel y Ci in a south to south-easterly direction. Eventually, this flattens somewhat until a wall and gate is reached at **G.R.642655**. Superb views here of Bethesda and the Ogwen Valley in the distance.

2. Now head uphill in a northerly direction to the summit of Moel y Ci, following a narrow footpath through the heather. On reaching the top, continue to the Trig. Point at 396m. Stay on the steeply descending path, which is rocky in places with occasional tussocks to point **G.R.586664**. Here the path intersects with the rough track you have just run up previously from Rallt Uchaf. Turn right (north easterly) and run along the path towards the obvious conifer woods now ahead of you. Enter the woods and run along the delightful track (tree roots – care!) downhill to **G.R. 593667**. Turn sharp right here and head back up hill for a short distance through the trees until a descending, stony, wet track is reached. This descends from a dwelling marked as 'Bwlchdefeity' on the map. Run down this track until you reach (once again!) the tarmac road you ran along earlier. Turn right here and retrace your route back to Moel y Ci Farm. However, at point **G.R. 596676**, turn right along a vague, sometimes muddy, track which, after a short distance, connects with a more defined track that heads westwards back to Moel y Ci Farm and, hence, marks the finish of this great little run.

DOLGARROG 'PIPE DREAM'
ROUTE 6

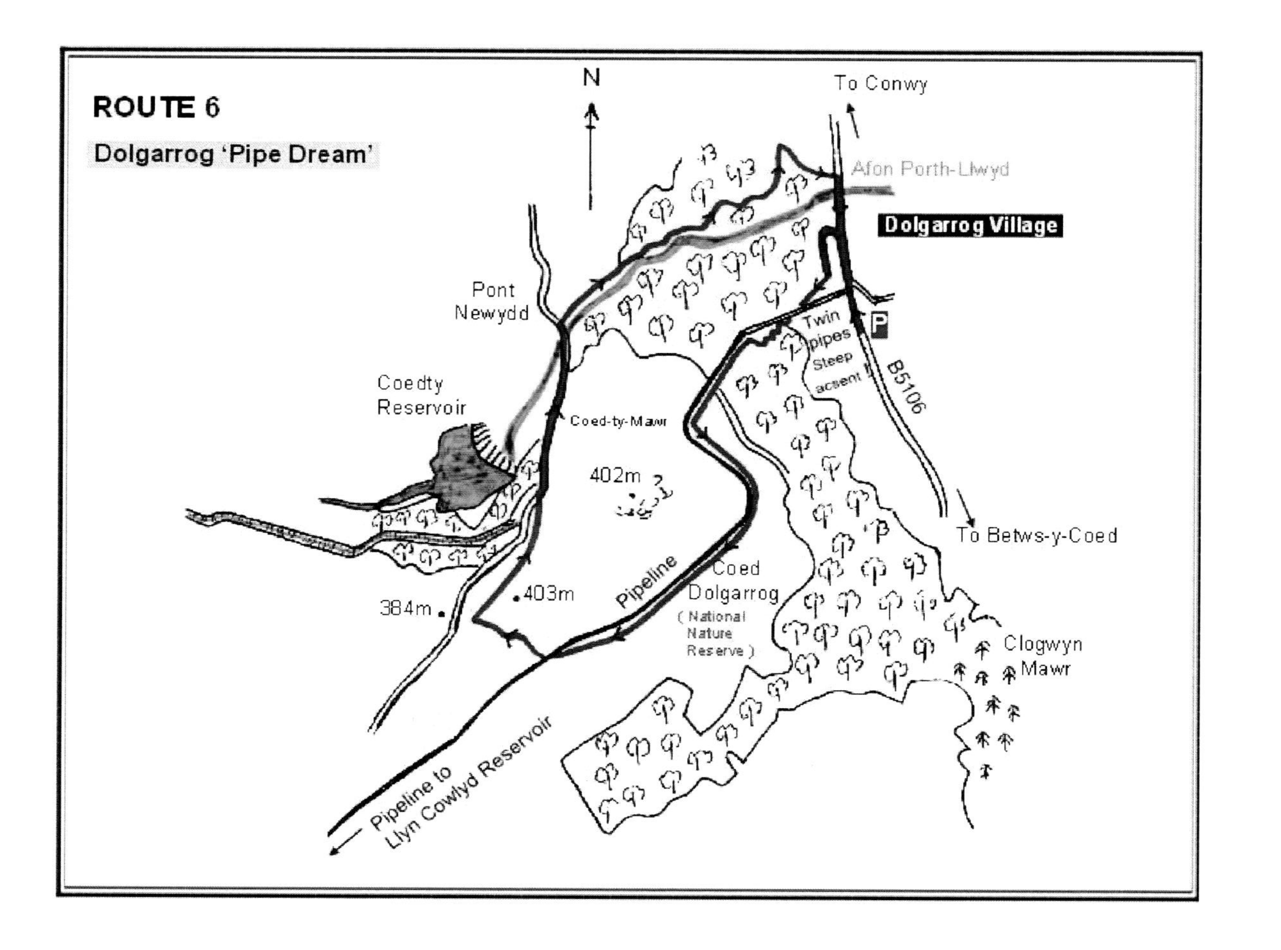

ROUTE 6
Dolgarrog 'Pipe Dream'
N
To Conwy
Afon Porth-Llwyd
Dolgarrog Village
P
Twin pipes
Steep acsent
B5106
To Betws-y-Coed
Pont Newydd
Coedty Reservoir
Coed-ty-Mawr
402m
403m
384m
Pipeline
Coed Dolgarrog
(National Nature Reserve)
Clogwyn Mawr
Pipeline to Llyn Cowlyd Reservoir

ROUTE 6: DOLGARROG 'PIPE DREAM'

DISTANCE: 5 Miles.
ASCENT: Min. 30metres @ start. Max. 403 metres.
TERRAIN: A mixture of woodland and open moorland gives this run a varied feel. A large proportion of the route follows the two huge steel water pipes that span across the moors from Llyn Cowlyd Reservoir, descending very steeply down the hillside to finish in Dolgarrog. These can be viewed from the village, with the starting point a couple of hundred metres north of where they pass under the main road.
TIME: Allowing for route finding, anything between 40 minutes and one hour would very good.
START: Dolgarrog Village, Vale of Conwy.
O.S MAP: 1:25,000 Sheet North Wales OL17.
GRADIENT: Very steep initial ascent alongside 2 huge steel water pipes. After this the gradient eases to give a relatively flat, enjoyable run.
ACCESS: No access issues or restrictions.

Grid References

769676	Left turn into minor road off the B5106.
765670	280m contour and easy-angled track.
763659	Tal-isaf-ardda.
754661	Right turn across hillside.
757667	Farm track.
758672	Pont Newydd.

FGS Grading: Grading is F5 [D0, N1, T0, R1, H3]

Distance	**0**	Up to 6 miles
Navigation	**1**	Basic navigation skills needed
Terrain	**0**	75% + on graded track or path
Remoteness	**1**	Countryside in fairly close proximity to habitation – at least 80% of the route within 2 miles
Height	**3**	Over 250 ft per mile

A big turnout of runners at the start of the annual Dolgarrog Pipe Dream Race held every March. Photo by Julia Kelly.

Route Description :

1. From Dolgarrog village, run a short distance along the B5106 in a northerly direction. You cannot fail to notice the huge, steel, twin water pipes, steeply descending the hillside as they pass under the pavement and road itself. At **GR 769676**, turn left and into a minor tarmac road that gently ascends passing residential houses. At its end, head rightwards and run up a rough woodland track towards the huge metal water pipes.

2. Now take on the 'daunting' prospect of running up the hillside adjacent to the water pipes. Beginning at approximately the 20m contour, this very steep ascent continues all the way to the 280m contour… all in a distance of just over ½ mile! Assuming you have reached the top at **GR 765670**, follow the relatively easy angled track that heads in a southerly direction for a short distance. Take a right turn and run along the narrow footpath that follows the pipeline (now horizontal!) in a south westerly direction.

3. Just above Tal- isaf- ardda (**GR 763659**) go under the pipeline and run gently uphill along a defined, wide farm track. At **GR 754661**, near to the 384m spot height, take a right turn across the grassy hillside towards the 403m height. Descend the grassy slope to join another farm track at **GR 757667**.

4. Run along this track passing 'Coed - ty – mawr' down to 'Pont Newydd' at **GR 758672**. At Pont Newydd, locate a descending public footpath just after the River, 'Afon Porth Llwyd'. Follow this as it descends steeply through trees above the river. At the 30m contour the path connects with the B5106. Turn right and run along the pavement back to your starting point in Dolgarrog Village.

MOEL WNION
ROUTE 7

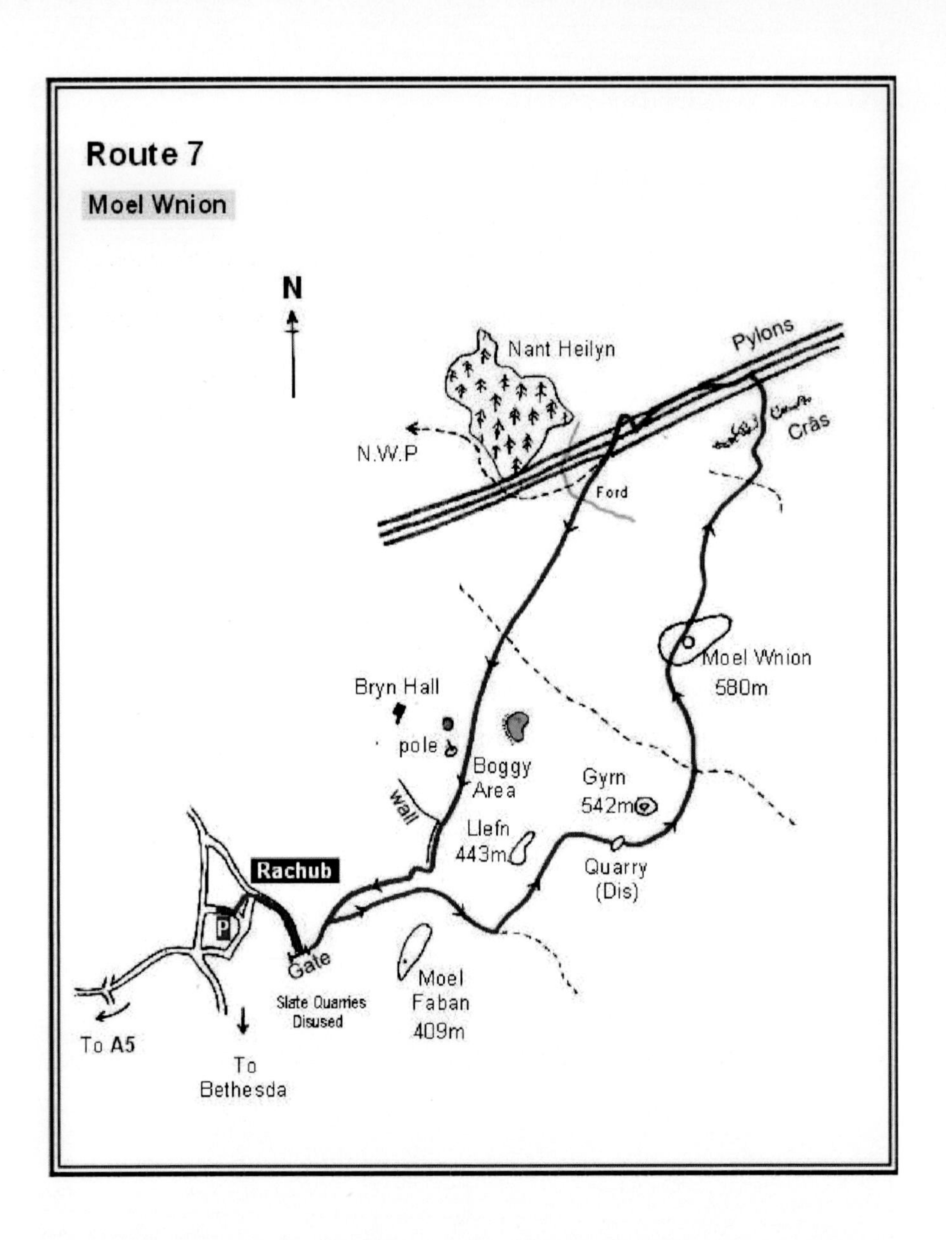

Route 7
Moel Wnion
N
Nant Heilyn
Pylons
N.W.P
Ford
Crâs
Moel Wnion
580m
Bryn Hall
pole
Boggy
Area
Gyrn
542m
wall
Llefn
443m
Quarry
(Dis)
Rachub
P
Gate
Slate Quarries
Disused
Moel
Faban
409m
To A5
To
Bethesda

ROUTE 7: MOEL WNION

DISTANCE: 6.5 Miles
ASCENT: Min.180 metres @ start. Max.580 metres.
TERRAIN: Mostly on defined grassy paths with occasional stony sections. After prolonged rain, much of this route can become quite soggy, especially where surface streams are present. Although uphill all the way to the summit of Moel Wnion, none of the route is excessively steep. However, the landscape is quite 'featureless in places. In the event of low cloud or mist, route finding may pose a problem. Therefore, it is advised that a map and compass are taken along with the skills to use them.
TIME: 1Hr.30mins – 2Hrs. depending on stops etc.
START: At village of Rachub, Nr. Bethesda, by the village recreation field.
O.S MAP: 1:25,000 Sheet North Wales OL17.
GRADIENT: Long, gradual but steady slopes in ascent and descent. No excessively steep sections.
ACCESS: No known access issues.

Grid References

624683	Parking adjacent to Rachub Village Recreation Field
628680	Metal gate into old quarries
630682	Fork in the footpath
639682	Junction of footpaths towards Llefn
646686	Disused quarry
650690	Start of footpath towards Moel Wnion summit
649697	Moel Wnion summit cairn
654709	Crâs
646708	North Wales Path
645705	'Ford' across stream
639698	'Crossroads' of footpaths
636687	Corner of drystone wall

FGS Grading: Grading is F8 [D1, N2, T1, R2, H2]

Distance	**1**	6 – 12 miles
Navigation	**2**	Competent navigation skills needed
Terrain	**1**	50 – 75% on graded track or path. 25 – 50% off track.
Remoteness	**2**	Countryside not in close proximity to habitation – less than 20% of the route within 2 miles.
Height	**2**	Over 125ft per mile.

The Author, Jim Kelly running past the disused quarry at GR 646686, with Llefn in the background. Photo by Julia Kelly.

Route Description :

Rising to 580 metres, Moel Wnion sits on the north western fringe of Snowdonia National Park. Its rounded, grassy bulk can be viewed easily as one drives along the 55 Coast Road between Abergwyngregyn and Tal y Bont.

1. Begin this popular run in the village of Rachub, near Bethesda. Park adjacent to the recreation field at **GR 624683**. Run slightly uphill along the tarmac road until a kissing gate on the left allows access across a small grassy field. Run in a diagonal direction to another gate by a house. This emerges on to another short section of tarmac road which rises up towards some old disused slate quarries. At **GR 628680** yet another metal gate is reached. Go through this and turn immediately left and follow the steep grassy path in a north easterly direction. At **GR 630682** this path splits. Take the right hand fork as it climbs up the lower slope of Moel Faban (409m). Continue running along this as it gets steeper. Eventually, at **GR 639682** this path descends and connects with a smaller, less-defined path which travels in the direction of Llefn (443m) and the grey, rocky peak of Gryn (542m). A landmark here is the old disused quarry at **GR 646686**.

2. Continue along the narrow path as it proceeds northwards, crossing another footpath at **GR 650690**. Now begin the long, gradual ascent of Moel Wnion, taking a vague path through bilberry, heather and grass towards its summit cairn at 580m (**GR 649697**). From here, descend in a northerly direction towards Crâs at **GR 654709**, heading towards a clearly visible line of electricity pylons...visibility permitting, of course!

3. At the pylons (please note this is the same line of pylons encountered on the 'Aber Falls' run, Route 1!), run directly underneath them until one reaches a sheep pen in the corner of a walled field. Take the ladder stile on the right and descend a short way until the North Wales Path is met at **GR 646708**. Run along this a short distance, passing a gate, until a left fork takes one towards a stream 'gully'. A convenient large boulder acts as a point at which to 'ford' the stream (**GR 645705**). After a metal stile over the wall, locate a vague path through gorse bushes until a much better, narrow, cairned path is found, leading you in a south westerly direction back towards Rachub. At **GR 639698** a conspicuous junction/crossroads of paths is met. Continue running straight over across a normally wet, boggy area where, once again, the path isn't entirely clear. Low gorse bushes also make progress a touch more tricky here. A landmark is a large round slate shelter with a telegraph pole sticking out of it! Stay left of and upslope of this. Run towards to corner of a wall at **GR 636687**.

4. At the corner of the wall the path becomes drier and more defined. Remain on this until the iron gate at the disused slate quarries is met yet again. Go through this once more and retrace your steps down the track/tarmac road towards Rachub and the recreation field starting point.

Descending from Moel Wnion towards the line of electricity pylons near Crâs.
Photo by Julia Kelly.

MOEL TRYFAN
ROUTE 8

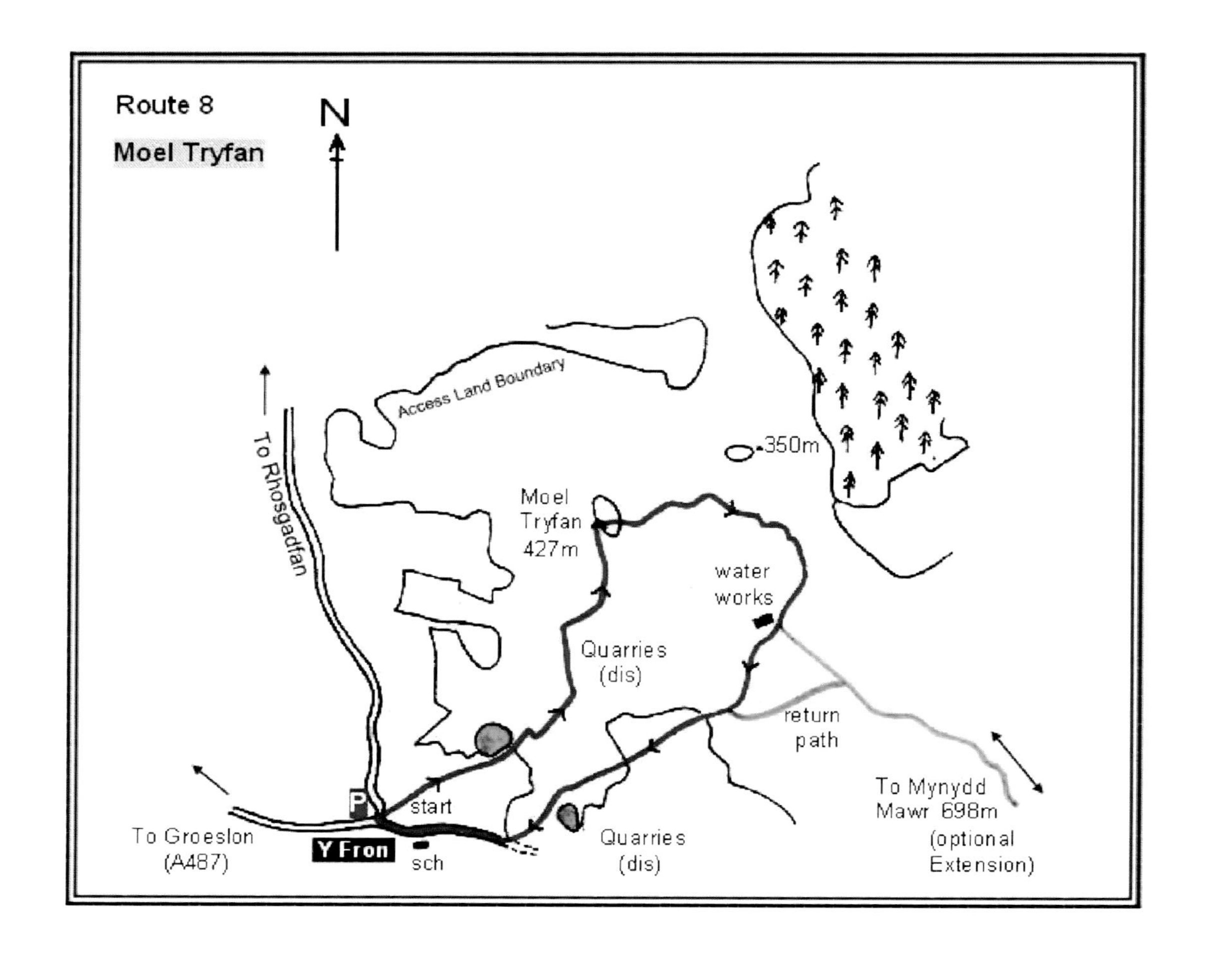

Route 8
Moel Tryfan
N
To Rhosgadfan
Access Land Boundary
350m
Moel Tryfan 427m
water works
Quarries (dis)
return path
To Groeslon (A487)
P
start
Y Fron
sch
Quarries (dis)
To Mynydd Mawr 698m (optional Extension)

ROUTE 8: MOEL TRYFAN

DISTANCE: 3.1Miles (or, 5.7miles with extension up 'Mynydd Mawr')
ASCENT: Min.292 metres @ start. Max.427 metres (698m if extended).
TERRAIN: From the start of the run defined tracks and paths are used until one reaches the disused slate quarries. Here the route becomes less defined and more rocky as it climbs to the summit. The descent is quite fast and, at times, can be quite wet and 'soggy' over heather/ peat moorland. If one opts to tackle the extension up Mynydd Mawr expect a sustained, steep climb over moorland grass, surface rocks and heather tussocks.
TIME: Depending on ability, anything from sub 20 minutes to 25 minutes to complete this run. If Mynydd Mawr is included, add a further 40 to 50 minutes to the run.
START: Y Fron Village.
O.S MAP: 1:25,000 Sheet North Wales OL17.
GRADIENT: A steady climb to the top of Moel Tryfan followed by a fast, steep descent. Mynydd Mawr is continually steep and sustained as it climbs from the 340m contour to its summit at 698m.
ACCESS: No access restrictions with the majority of the route running on Access Land.

Grid References

506549	Parking in the village of Y Fron.
515563	Summit of Moel Tryfan.
522563	Junction between track and quarry path.
523558	Water Works.
520553	Finishing point.
540547	Summit of Mynydd Mawr (optional).
525556	Return footpath to Y Fron.

FGS Grading: Grading is F6 (F8*) D0(1), N1(1), T1(1),R2(2),H3(3) ****indicates optional extension route.***

Distance	0 (1)	Up to 6 miles (6 – 12 miles)
Navigation	**1 (1)**	Basic navigation skills needed.
Terrain	**1 (1)**	50 – 75% on graded track or path 25 – 50% off track.
Remoteness	**1 (2)**	Countryside in fairly close proximity to habitation – at least 80% of the route within 2 miles. (Countryside not in close proximity – less than 20% of the route within 2 miles).
Height	**3 (3)**	Over 250 ft per mile.

Runners in the final stage of the annual Moel Tryfan race. Photo by Julia Kelly.

Route Description :

A short but fierce little route that features as one of the ERYRI Harriers' more popular races early on in the annual events calendar. Being a fast route, it is reasonable to expect anytime between sub 20 minutes as 'excellent' with 20 to 28 minutes more the average. In wet weather, the latter part of the run can get quite soggy so, expect wet feet!

1. Park in the village of Y Fron at **GR 506549** where there is a flat, open area of land. From here a gravel track rises gently past fields with a slate quarry lake on your left **GR 512553**. This path continues north easterly over some softer ground until another slate quarry track is joined. This heads upwards towards where it narrows through some slate blocks and scree piles. After a short climb over open country, the rocky top of Moel Tryfan (427m) can be seen dead ahead. At the top (**GR 515563**), descend in an easterly direction following a fast, vague, downhill path which eventually meets an old quarry road.

2. Follow this road to where it meets a small footpath that skirts the piles of slate **GR 522563**. Run this downhill, eventually connecting with a much more defined path that heads south west towards the Water Works at **GR 523558**. Continue running along this until you reach the works. Now take a left fork down a vague track across heather which connects with an old tarmac road heading back towards Y Fron Village and, at **GR520553**, your finishing point.

UNLESS of course you wish to extend this run! If so, read on......
It is possible to link Moel Tryfan with its much larger neighbour, 'Mynydd Mawr' (698m) / **GR 540547**.

3. At the water works, locate and follow an ever steepening footpath through heather and surface stones all the way to its broad summit. Now retrace your steps for the fast descent, joining a track at

GR 52556 which leads you back to Y Fron village. This pleasant extension adds a further 2.6 miles in distance and approximately 40 to 50 minutes in time.

Mynydd Mawr as viewed from the village of Y Fron. The extension run takes the left hand skyline. (Photo by Julia Kelly.

MYNYDD MAWR
ROUTE 9

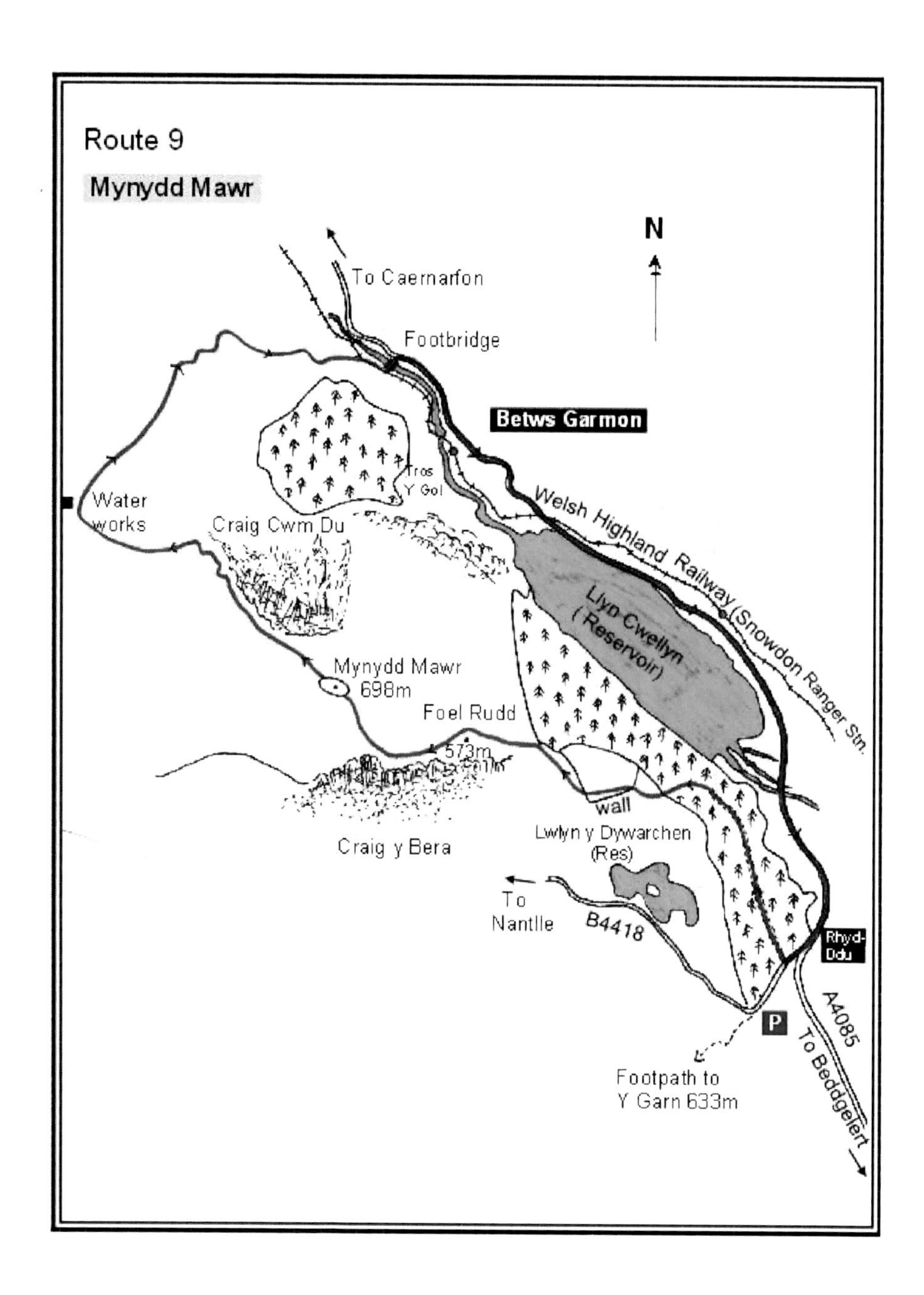
Route 9
Mynydd Mawr
N
To Caernarfon
Footbridge
Betws Garmon
Tros Y Gol
Water works
Craig Cwm Du
Welsh Highland Railway (Snowdon Ranger Stn.
Llyn Cwellyn (Reservoir)
Mynydd Mawr 698m
Foel Rudd
573m
wall
Craig y Bera
Lwlyn y Dywarchen (Res)
To Nantlle
B4418
Rhyd-Ddu
P
A4085
To Beddgelert
Footpath to Y Garn 633m

ROUTE 9: MYNYDD MAWR

DISTANCE: 9.5 Miles
ASCENT: Min. 204 metres @ start. Max. 698 metres.
TERRAIN: A pleasant mix of trail, open country, steep mountain ascent and road make this run one of the more varied in this guide. Some sections, particularly on the descent to Betws Garmon, are prone to wetness' and can become quite marshy after heavy or prolonged rain. Expect wet feet! The views throughout, on a clear day, are outstanding.
TIME: 1hr 45m – 2hrs 15m
START: Roadside layby on B4418 slightly south west of Rhyd Ddu at GR 567526.
O.S MAP: 1:25,000 Sheet North Wales OL17.
GRADIENT: Steep ascent from Beddgelert forest section to the summit of Mynydd Mawr. Long gradual descent from the summit, reducing in gradient all the time.
ACCESS: Run is all on public paths, tracks and roads. No known access problems or restrictions.

Grid References

567536	Beddgelert forest
562540	Open Country
554544	Stile
532556	Path divides
530559	Ford
535569	Tyddyn Bach
542567	Welsh Highland Railway

FGS Grading: Grading is F9 [D1, N2, T1, R2, H3]

Distance	**1**	6 – 12 miles.
Navigation	**2**	Competent navigation skills needed.
Terrain	**1**	50 – 75% on graded track or path. 25 -50% off track.
Remoteness	**2**	Countryside not in close proximity to habitation – less than 20% of the route within 2 miles.
Height	**3**	Over 250 ft per mile.

Route Description :

Park along the roadside at **GR 567526**. This is a short way south west of the village of Rhyd Ddu on the B4418. It is the 'normal' place to park if going for a walk or run up the nearby Y Garn or, the longer, Nantlle Ridge.

1. From here, run a short distance back down towards the village. Just before the road junction with the A4085, take an obvious left turn up a well-defined forestry track, signed 'Rhydd Ddu Welcome'. This leads in a northerly direction through what is termed 'Beddgelert Forest' (**GR 562543**). Eventually, this track diminishes in size and forms a narrow rising footpath up hill through the pine trees and out onto open country at **GR 562540**. Remain on this path over scrub and grassland, passing two drystone walls.

Jim Kelly about to tackle the steep section leading to the top of Foel Rudd at 573 metres. Photo by Julia Kelly.

2. At the second wall and stile, climb the hillside near to the wall ending up, eventually, at another stile at the top corner of the woodland (**GR 554544**). From here, the gradient increases significantly as a steep, broken path leads up to Foel Rudd at 573 metres.

Almost at the top of Foel Rudd after the steep ascent. Photo by Julia Kelly.

Thankfully, this path flattens somewhat as it curves its way, high above Craig y Bera, towards the rocky summit cairn of Mynydd Mawr at 698 metres. On a clear day, the views from this position are superb!

At the top, the descent follows a vague path/line down Mynydd Mawr's blunt northern spur.

This consists of steep grass, heather and surface stones towards Moel Tryfan (see previous Route 8!). At **GR 532556** the path splits (small low cairn). Take the narrow right fork downhill until you reach the point marked 'ford' at **GR 530559**.

3. This area drains the upper slopes and can become quite wet. Cross over to a wall and follow the path alongside the wall. After a short way you will see a public footpath sign and a gate on your right. Go through this, running down a worn path in a north easterly direction towards the area marked as 'Betws Garmon'. At one point, the path descends to small stream. Cross this and go through a gap in the wall marked by 2 rusty metal posts. Turn immediately left and locate the path which descends through the pine woods (care with exposed tree roots!). Your descent continues pleasantly through trees and across pasture land to arrive at 'Tyddyn-Bach' (**GR 535569**). Here, turn right onto a farm track

and fields, marked by signs and stiles. This marshy section heads east, passing, eventually, over the 'Welsh Highland Railway' track at **GR 542567**. Watch out for steam trains! Although the train is relatively slow moving, don't get run over by it! After a very short distance, the path crosses a footbridge over the Afon Gwyrfai that feeds the reservoir of Llyn Cwellyn (**GR 560550**).

4. By complete contrast, the remaining 3 miles of this route now follows the main A4085 road back to the village of Rhyd Ddu, with Llyn Cwellyn, delightfully, on your right hand side. It is worth noting here that this valley road forms part of the annual Snowdonia Marathon route (Beddgelert to Waunfawr Section), held at the end of each October. However, on reaching Rhyd Ddu village once again, be assured that you will arrive at your car in a slightly more 'comfortable state' than the 2000 or so competitors who sign-up to take part in the tortuous 26 mile marathon event that passes through this spot each year! Now there's a challenge!! (logon to: *www.snowdoniamarathon.com*)

CARNEDDAU CIRCUIT
ROUTE 10

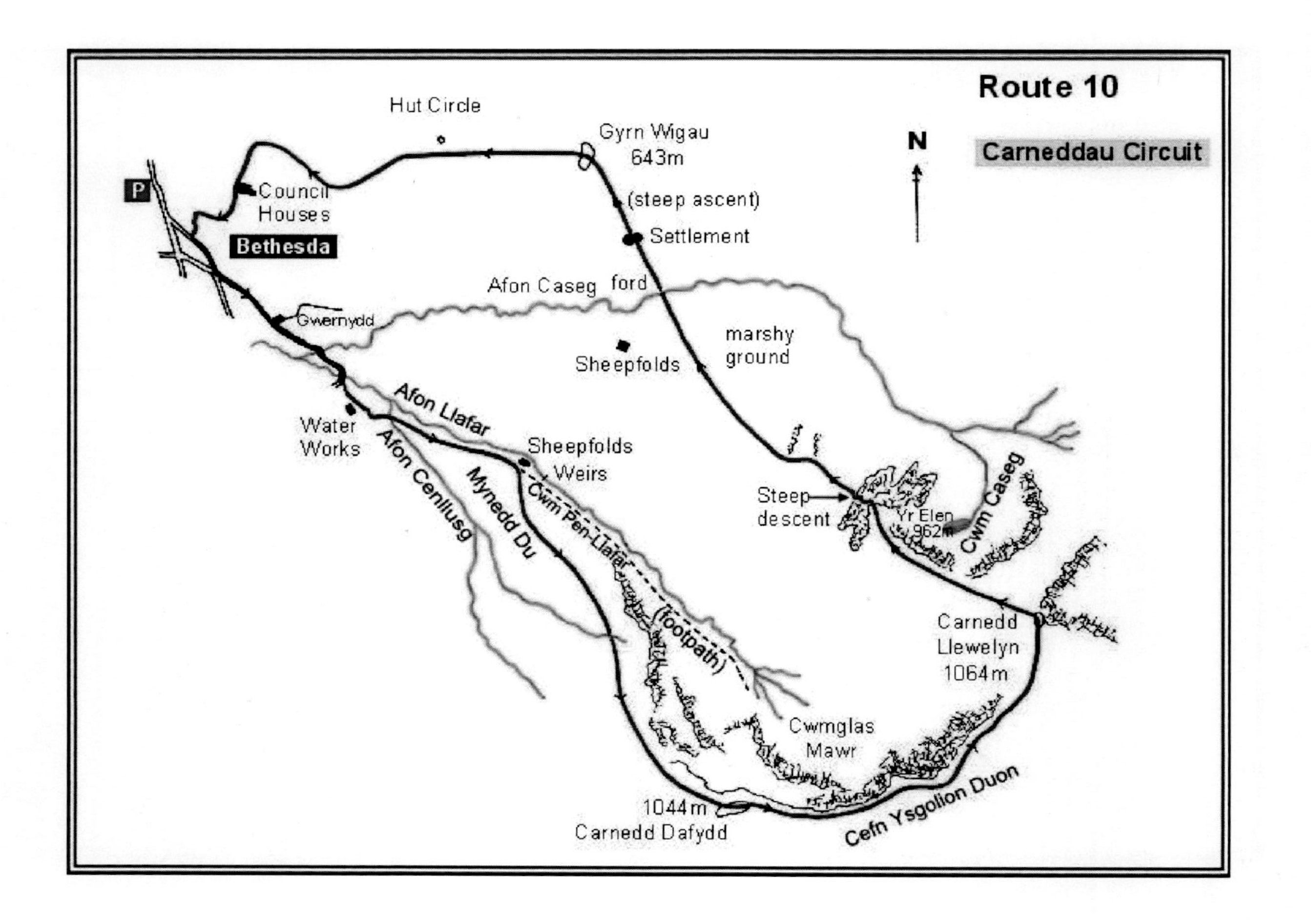

Route 10
Carneddau Circuit
N
Hut Circle
Gyrn Wigau
643m
(steep ascent)
Settlement
P
Council
Houses
Bethesda
Afon Caseg
ford
Gwernydd
Sheepfolds
marshy
ground
Afon Llafar
Water
Works
Afon Cenllusg
Mynedd Du
Sheepfolds
Weirs
Cwm Pen-Llafar
(footpath)
Steep
descent
Yr Elen
962m
Cwm Caseg
Carnedd
Llewelyn
1064m
Cwmglas
Mawr
1044m
Carnedd Dafydd
Cefn Ysgolion Duon

ROUTE 10: CARNEDDAU CIRCUIT

DISTANCE: 9.2 Miles
ASCENT: Min.180 metres @ start. Max.1064 metres.
TERRAIN: This route includes some of the highest peaks in the Carneddau area and, as a result, it is a demanding run requiring a high degree of fitness and navigation skills. This is particularly important if one gets caught out in poor weather conditions/visibility. Much of it is run on undefined paths which vary between surface stones and concealed rocks to grass/ bulrush tussocks over very marshy, valley terrain. In addition to this, some very steep unrelenting slopes are climbed and descended (total ascent 4,200 ft), making this a mountain run of considerable character and seriousness with a remote feel to it. It is highly advisable to carry a hydration pack with full mountain running kit and 1 – 1 ½ litres of fluid on board. During the autumn and winter the lower sections on both ascent and descent can get very wet and boggy. Expect a thorough soaking!
TIME: 2 – 2 ½ hours average. Under 2 hours is very good.
START: 'Gwernydd', Bethesda. (GR 635663)
O.S MAP: 1:25,000 Sheet North Wales OL17.
GRADIENT: Long steep ascents and descents up some of the highest mountains in Snowdonia.
ACCESS: No known access issues.

Grid References

625672	Roadside parking in Bethesda.
635663	'Gwernydd' official starting place for the race.
639657	Water works.
648654	Footpath towards Mynydd Du.
663661	Carnedd Dafydd summit.
684645	Carnedd Llewelyn summit.
674651	Yr Elen .
671655	Braich y Llyngwm.
657688	Old settlement.
653675	Gyrn Wigau summit.
645676	Gallt y Mawn
639682	Junction of less-defined path.

FGS Grading: Grading is F13 [D1, N3, T3, R3, H3]

Distance	**1**	6 – 12 miles
Navigation	**3**	Expert navigation skills needed
Terrain	**3**	Under 25% on graded track or path. Over 75% off track.
Remoteness	**3**	Remote, isolated location.
Height	**3**	Over 250 ft per mile.

Fording the Afon Cenllusg.

Route Description :

1. Park in the village of Bethesda. A good location is at **GR 625672** by the King George Pub. From here, walk or run to the 'official' start at Gwernydd (**GR 635663**). Run along the minor road towards the water works at **GR 639657**, crossing over the Afon Caseg and the Afon Llafar. At the sharp right bend, ignore the first path on the left marked with a sign. Instead, continue to run a short distance taking a left turn off the minor road, following a track passing the water works which connects with a public footpath that crosses some fields. After a short distance, the main footpath ascending towards Cwm Pen Llafar is met (the Afon Llafar is on your left hand side here). The grassy path is marked with grey wooden marker posts all the way here and can get quite wet in these lower sections. Cross the small stream known as Afon Cenllusg and

Running up the steep grassy spur of 'Mynydd Du' with Yr Elen in the background.

follow the path towards a stile in the wall. After another wall at **GR 648654**, break out right from the footpath and tackle the steep slope of Mynydd Du, following a less defined path in a south easterly direction, running over open country. This flattens briefly before the slope 'kicks in' once again and heads southerly towards Foel Merich. Rocky, steep terrain from here leads one to the summit cairns of Carnedd Dafydd at 1044m (**GR 663631**).

2. You now have a short respite as the route follows the well-defined walkers' footpath that runs along the edge of the 'rim' above Cefn Ysgolion Duon with the vertical Black Ladders cliffs below you. Continue running over rocks, boulders and grass as this path gradually rises towards the higher, Carnedd Llewelyn at 1064m (**GR 684645**). A steep, scree covered path leads to its rounded summit and large cairn. At

Looking up towards the steep slope of 'Carnedd Dafydd' and the 'Black Ladders'.

the cairn run north westerly towards Yr Elen (962m) at **GR 674651**. In poor weather take care here as steep rocks and cliffs drop down to Cwm Caseg which is on your right hand side. At Yr Elen, proceed north westerly and follow the very steep zig-zag path that descends through loose rocks and scree. At its base, around the 800m contour, head down steep grassland marked on the OS Map as Braich y-Llyngwm (**GR 671655**). Your 'destination' here is the settlement on the other side of the valley at **GR 657668**. There is no defined path to follow and from Braich y Llyngwn the compass bearing is 322 degrees. This is normally a very wet section through saturated marshland, especially in the lower section as one approaches the Afon Caseg mountain stream.It is quite the 'norm' to be up to your calves/knees in water and bog! Nice! Locate a suitable place to 'ford' the stream and head up to the walls of the settlement. Above you looms the last great 'obstacle' – 'Gyrn Wigau' (643m) at **GR 653675**. In the annual Carneddau race, this is normally regarded as the 'killer section' with most competitors struggling to even walk up this... never mind run up it! Basically, it is 'head down, ignore the pain and yard it to the top' telling yourself, "It's all downhill after this!"

3. At the summit of Wigau, run due west down steep grass and tussocks towards the defined footpath marked as 'Gallt y Mawn' on the map (**GR 645676**). Pick up this footpath and head northwards towards Moel Faban (409m.).The path skirts around this on Faban's northern finge (Bwlch ym Mhwll-le). At **GR 639682** a less-defined path is met. Follow this taking a left turn south westerly back towards Bethesda. This path joins a better track/road after a little distance. Stay on this passing 'Gilfodan' (**GR 628671**). At the T-junction turn right and your car (and the pub!!) is only a few long strides away.

MOEL-Y-GEST
ROUTE 11

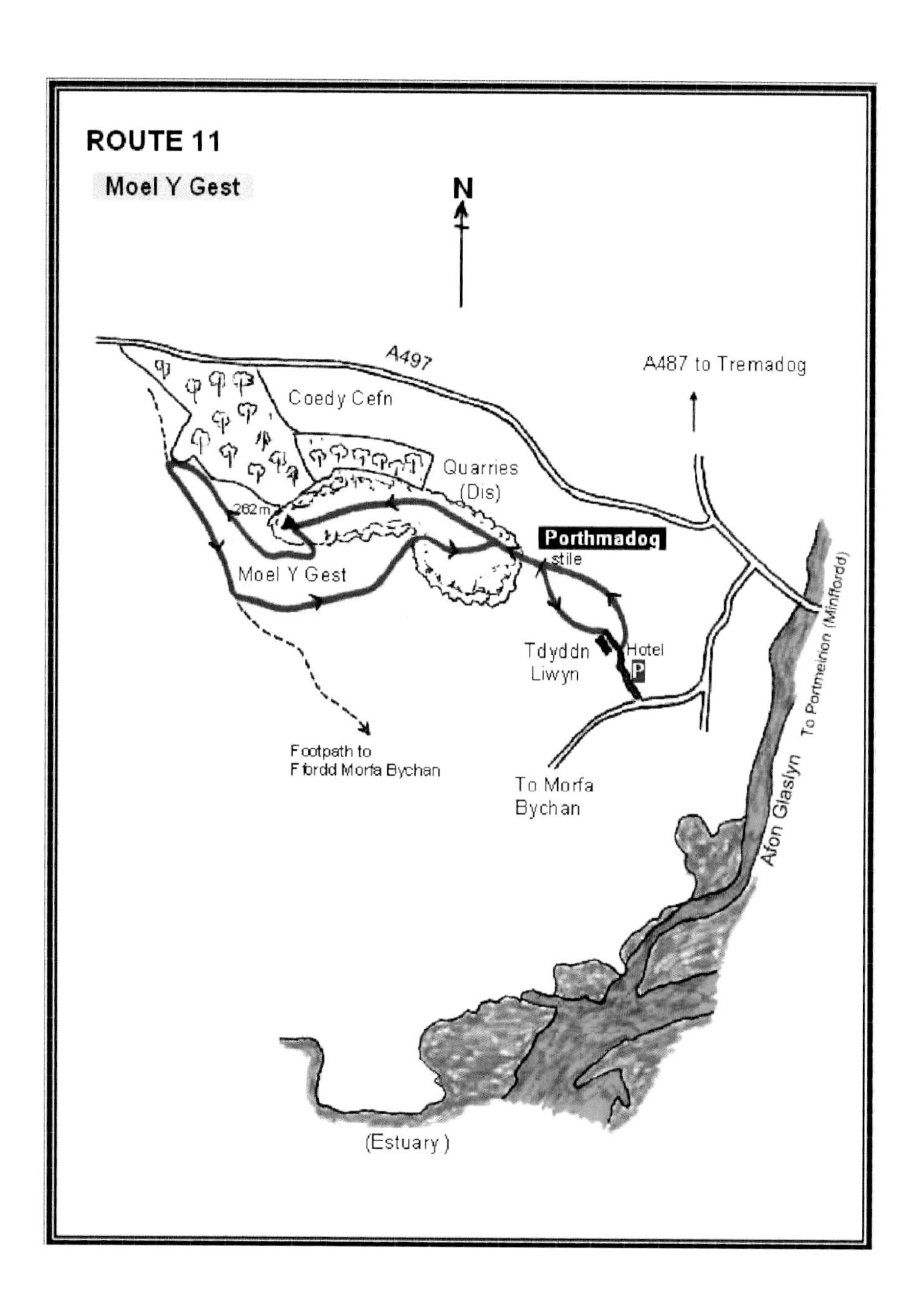
ROUTE 11
Moel Y Gest
N
A497
A487 to Tremadog
Coedy Cefn
Quarries
(Dis)
262m
Porthmadog
stile
Moel Y Gest
Tdyddn
Liwyn
Hotel
P
Footpath to
Ffordd Morfa Bychan
To Morfa
Bychan
To Portmeirion (Minffordd)
Afon Glaslyn
(Estuary)

ROUTE 11: MOEL-Y-GEST

DISTANCE: 3.2 Miles
ASCENT: Min.10 metres @ start. Max. 262 metres.
TERRAIN: Although short, this great little route packs quite a punch in terms of the effort required to complete it in a good time. It is run mainly on defined paths across steep, rocky, quarried ground and over rough grass/ moorland. Care is required on some of the loose, rocky, descent sections to ensure no twisted ankles! The initial section is getting overgrown by saplings and the occasional bramble bush. Try to avoid getting stung or impaled!
TIME: Average 40 – 50 minutes. Under 35 minutes is very good!
START: Tyddyn Llŵyn Touring Park/ Hotel (Nice bar and beer!).
O.S MAP: 1:25,000 Sheet North Wales OL18.
GRADIENT: Very steep climb from almost sea level to 262m in a short distance.
ACCESS: Although the access road to Tyddyn Llŵyn Campsite is a designated public footpath, it is only courteous to ask the owners of Tyddyn Llwyn Touring Park if it is ok to park and run there. The route over Moel y Gest is entirely on Access Land with no known restrictions other than a request to keep dogs on a lead.

Grid References

563384 Start at Tyddyn Llwyn Campsite/ Hotel.
560387 Convergence of paths and stile.
555388 Secondary summit at 231m.
549389 Moel y Gest main summit/ trig point at 262m.
545392 Public footpath.

FGS Grading: Grading is F7 [D0, N1, T2, R1, H3]

Distance	0	Up To 6 miles.
Navigation	1	Basic navigation skills needed.
Terrain	2	25 – 50% on graded track or path 25 –50% off track.
Remoteness	1	Countryside in fairly close proximity to habitation – at least 80% of the route within 2 miles.
Height	3	Over 250 ft per mile.

Route Description :

1. From the tarmac parking area in front of the reception office run a short distance back towards the site entrance and turn immediately left through a gate and onto a gently rising stony track. This is also sign-marked as a public footpath. Follow this past some piles of building debris until it forks rightwards up a short bank and continues uphill through grass, bracken and bushes. Take care here as there are also low brambles and branches. After a short distance a wall and ladder stile is met at **GR 560387**. Hop over this and continue steeply up a narrow, rocky path to another stile. Go over this and follow the path up through trees over steep rocks and stones to the lower summit at 231m. (**GR 555388**). From here, the vague path descends slightly, heading

Approaching the lower summit of Moel y Gest (231m). The camping site of Tyddyn Llwyn can be seen below along with the stunning views across the Porthmadog Estuary (Photo: Julia Kelly).

westwards, towards the high point of Moel y Gest and its trig point at 262m. (**GR 549389**)

2. At the top, drop steeply down the southerly side and follow the intermittent path downhill in a west-north westerly direction across grass and tussocks until it reaches a more defined path heading towards 'Bron y Foel' on the map at **GR 545392**. Run along this good path for ¼ mile or so until a wall/ gate is reached at **GR 547387**. Now head uphill once more, gently at first, in an easterly direction across a boggy area towards another wall. Go over this and run steeply back towards the lower summit at 231m once again. By now the legs will be feeling it! Just hang in there because it is all downhill from here.

3. Retrace your steps downhill crossing the two earlier ladder stiles. At the lower stile, instead of turning left back through the bracken and brambles, head straight down through some trees, eventually emerging on some open ground that terminates at the upper end of Tyddyn Llwyn Caravan Site. Continue running along the tarmac road towards the hotel and, if you time it right, the sanctuary of the bar!

MOEL EILIO CIRCUIT
ROUTE 12

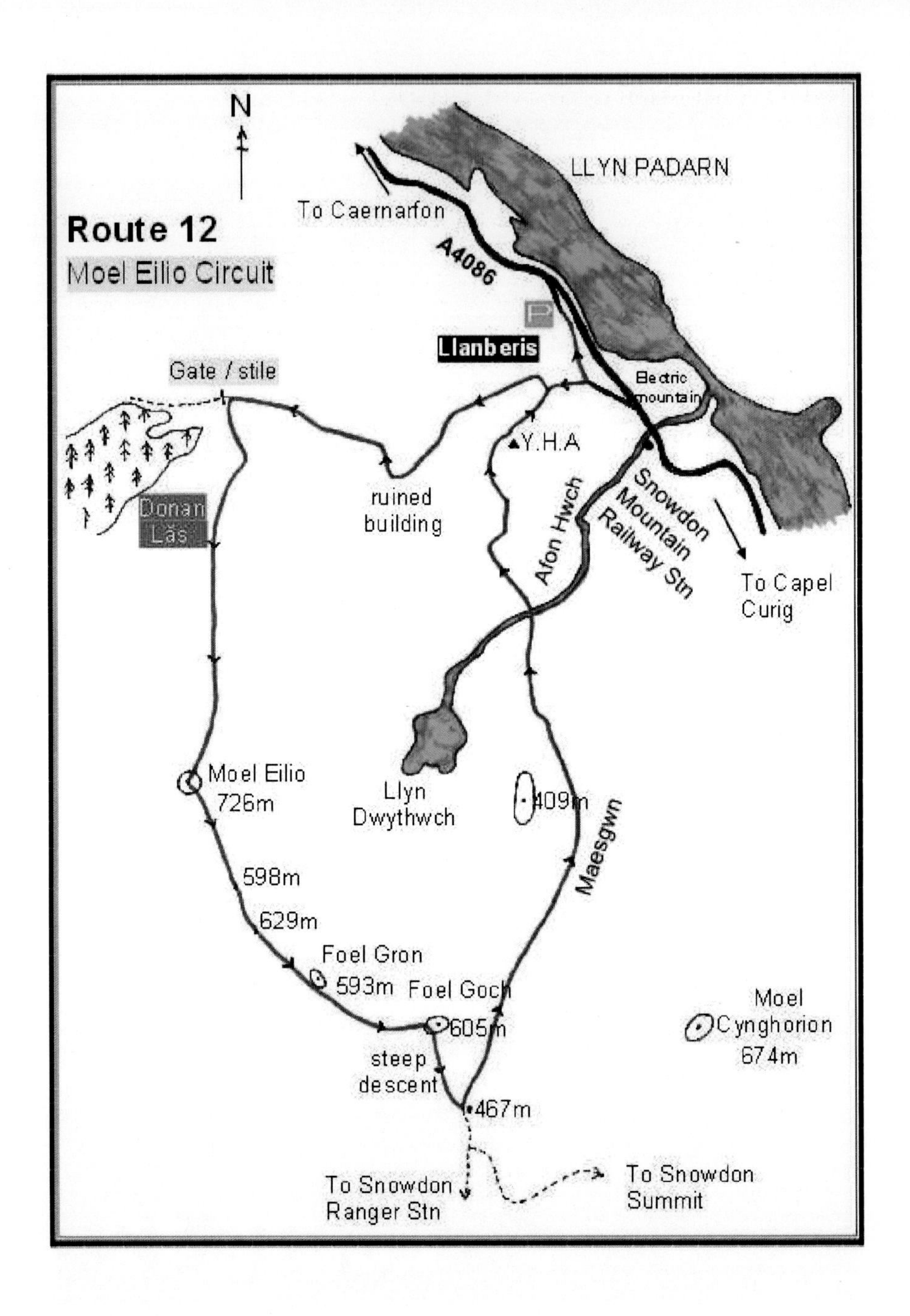
N
Route 12
Moel Eilio Circuit
LLYN PADARN
To Caernarfon
A4086
P
Llanberis
Gate / stile
Electric mountain
Y.H.A
ruined building
Donan Läs
Afon Hwch
Snowdon Mountain Railway Stn
To Capel Curig
Moel Eilio 726m
Llyn Dwythwch
409m
Maesgwn
598m
629m
Foel Gron
593m
Foel Goch
605m
Moel Cynghorion 674m
steep descent
467m
To Snowdon Ranger Stn
To Snowdon Summit

ROUTE 12: MOEL EILIO CIRCUIT

DISTANCE: 8.5 Miles
ASCENT: Min.109 metres @ start. Max. 726 metres.
TERRAIN: The run begins and finishes on tarmac roads in Llanberis. However, the section in between is 100% fell! Rough paths and tracks are punctuated with tussock grass, boggy areas and rocks. In addition to this, it's high and involves some long climbs and descents which, in places, are steep (and slippery when wet!). On a clear day, the views from the top and the ridge are superb! A classic training route and fell race.
TIME: 1 Hr 30 mins. approximately
START: Llanberis Village. Park at G.R. 576606 (opposite 'Coed y Glyn') or, in one of the many pay & display car parks. Beware of parking in the centre of the village itself. Wardens patrol and will impose fixed penalties for parking over the permitted times!
O.S MAP: 1:25,000 Sheet North Wales OL17.
GRADIENT: Sustained uphill sections, steep in places. Some steep descents.
ACCESS: The usual mixture of rights of way and open access land (see map).

Grid References

576606	Car parking in Llanberis opposite Coed y Glyn.
571601	Right turn up minor road (Ffordd Capel Coch) towards village school.
570598	Steep road section/ metal gate.
557599	Bwlch y Groes Quarry (Dis).
555587	Bryn Mawr.
560568	Spot height point 629m.
569564	Summit of Foel Goch @ 605m.
573558	Junction of footpaths at the top of Maesgwm 467m.
578573	Gate between path and rocky track.
575584	Ford Brithdir.
573591	Track joins minor road.

FGS Grading: Grading is F10 [D1, N2,T2, R2,H3]

Distance	**1**	6 – 12 miles
Navigation	**2**	Competent navigation skills needed.
Terrain	**2**	25 – 50% on graded track or path 25 –50% off track.
Remoteness	**2**	Countryside not in close proximity to Habitation – less than 20% of the route within 2 miles.
Height	**3**	Over 250 ft per mile.

Approaching the top of Foel Goch at 605m with Foel Gron and Moel Eilio in the far distance. Photo by Julia Kelly.

Route Description :

1. Run through Llanberis High Street until you reach **GR 571601**. Take a right turn into 'Ffordd Capel Coch' up towards the village school passing the library on your right. After a chapel turn right and follow the road uphill to a sharp left bend. Continue up this minor road passing a steep section at **GR 570598** and a metal road gate. Eventually, one passes a ruined house on the left marked as 'Maen-Llwyd-Isaf' on the O.S. Map. Here the minor road merges with a stony, sometimes muddy, path climbing steadily uphill, passing a stile and a gate. Run this in a westerly direction to **GR 557599** marked as, 'Bwlch-y-Groes Quarry (dis)'. Now take the rough steep path that heads in a southerly direction up Moel Eilio itself crossing the rough pasture/ moorland marked as 'Bryn Mawr' **GR 555587**. As you run past the 660m contour, the gradient increases considerably all the way up to its broad summit and wind shelter/ cairn at 726m.

Maesgwm upper section.

2. At the top, descend in a south easterly direction (compass bearing 123 degs./ SE) to Bwlch Cwm Cesig at 598m running past spot height 629m at **GR 560568** and on to Foel Gron at 593m. Here a steep grassy descent with exposed rocks drops down to the saddle between Foel Gron and Foel Goch. Of course, what goes down has to go up(!) and Foel Goch is now steeply ascended to its broad, grassy top at 605m (**GR 569564**). A stile here gives access to another steep, grassy descent to **GR 573558**. This point is very recognisable as it is at the head of the valley known as 'Maesgwm'. Several other ways lead off here towards Snowdon summit and down to Nant y Betws, in the next valley below. However, our direction is a north-north easterly one returning via Maesgwm to Llanberis.

3. The stony, narrow path descends gently for most of its length to **GR 578573** where a gate gives access to a wider, rocky man-made path.

Maesgwm lower section above Llanberis

Proceed along this track (good views of the Snowdon Mountain Railway to your right!) crossing Ford Brithdir at **GR 575584** and on to point **GR 573591** where the track connects with a minor road. Run down this passing the farm campsite of Hafod Lydan and the Y.H.A. building on the right. Eventually after ¼ mile or so you will recognise the old chapel you passed earlier, on your right. Now retrace your 'strides' through Llanberis Village to your car and a well-earned pint of tea in Pete's Eats!

CADAIR IDRIS CIRCUIT
ROUTE 13

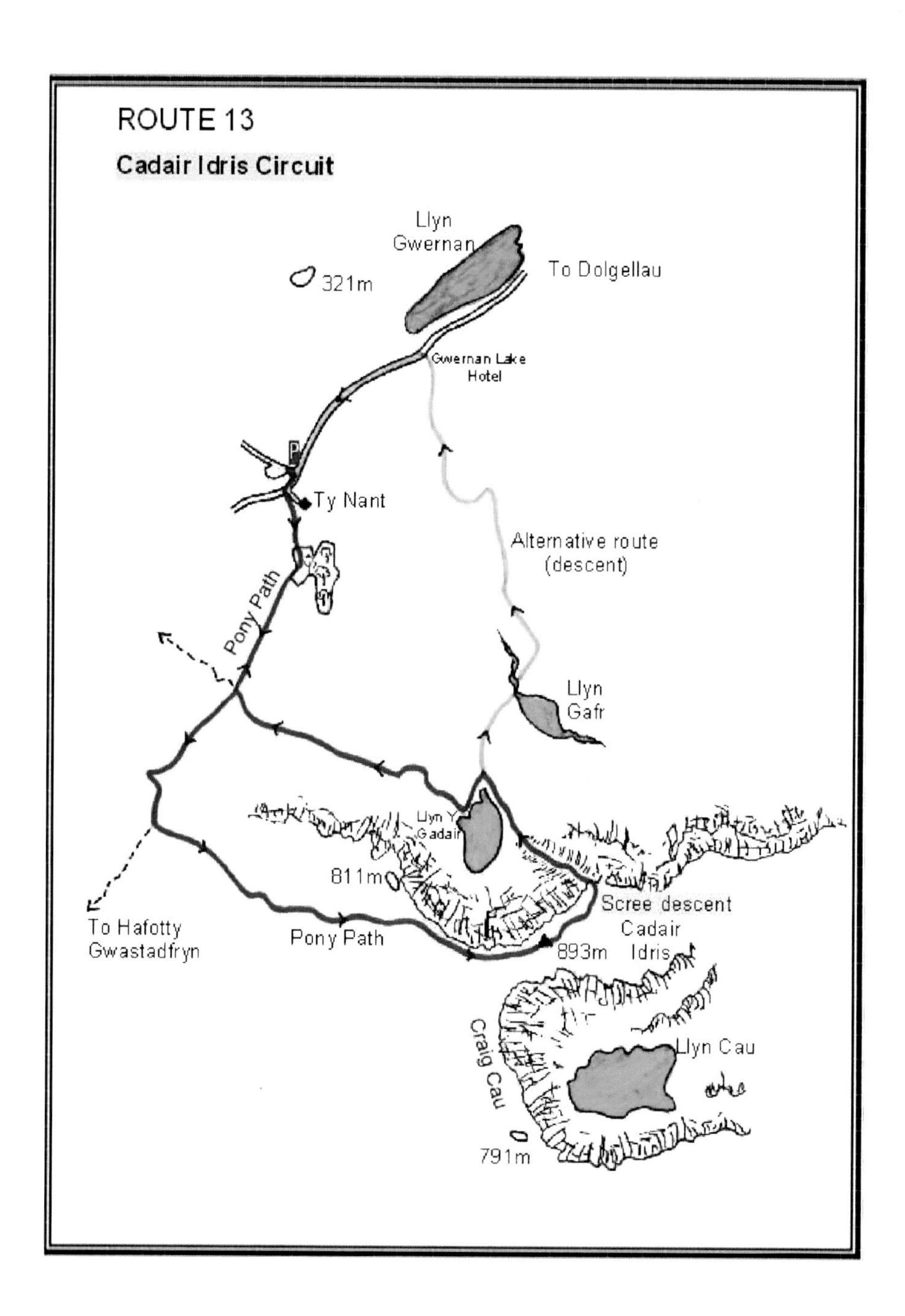
ROUTE 13
Cadair Idris Circuit
Llyn Gwernan
To Dolgellau
321m
Gwernan Lake Hotel
P
Ty Nant
Alternative route (descent)
Pony Path
Llyn Gafr
Llyn Y Gadair
811m
Scree descent
Cadair Idris
893m
To Hafotty Gwastadfryn
Pony Path
Craig Cau
Llyn Cau
791m

ROUTE 13: CADER IDRIS

DISTANCE: 5 Miles
ASCENT: Min.150 metres @ start. Max.893 metres.
TERRAIN: Cadair Idris ("The Chair of Idris" ...Idris being a legendary giant!) completely dominates the landscape for miles in every direction. On a clear day, almost all of Snowdonia can be viewed from its rocky summit. The majority of this route is on graded rocky footpaths very reminiscent of the "Llanberis Path" up Snowdon. The less defined sections require care particularly on the steep screes. Some areas of boggy ground over surface rocks and tussocks.
TIME: 1hr 30 – 45 minutes
START: Cadair Idris pay & display car park GR.698153
O.S MAP: 1:25,000 Sheet North Wales OL17.
GRADIENT: Steep in places with optional steep descent
ACCESS: No access issues but the whole area is a National Nature Reserve so please obey any signage.

Grid References

725179	Start of minor road in Dolgellau towards Cadair Idris.
705159	Gwernan Lake Hotel.
698153	Cadair Idris pay & display car park.
696143	Junction/ start of the 'Pony Path'.
718136	Llyn y Gadair
713133	Top of scree descent.
710141	Llyn Gafr.

FGS Grading: Grading is F7 [D0, N2, T1, R1, H3]

Distance	**0**	Up to 6 miles
Navigation	**2**	Competent navigation skills needed
Terrain	**1**	50 – 75% on graded track or path 25 - 50% off track
Remoteness	**1**	Countryside in fairly close proximity to habitation – at least 80% of the route within 2 miles
Height	**3**	Over 250ft per mile

Route Description :

1. From Dolgellau take a minor road (**GR 725179**) signposted "Cadair Idris". This is quite tricky to locate so do not be surprised if you circumnavigate Dolgellau's one-way traffic system more than once! Once located, follow this narrow valley road passing the Gwernan Lake Hotel on your right (GR 705159). Shortly after this, you will reach the National Trust pay & display car park at GR 698153. At the time of going to press, charges are set at £4 for the day and £2 for up to 4 hours.

2. From the car park, turn right and then 1st left up towards Ty Nant Farm and tea room. The track is well defined and rises quite steeply up engineered steps from the valley floor. After a short distance, one arrives at a junction (**GR 696143**), marked on the OS Map as the 'Pony Path'. Continue up this passing a steep section as the path takes a sharp right and then a left as it ascends the hillside.

At the sharp turn on the Pony Path before arriving at the col.
(Photo: Julia Kelly)

3. However, this is short-lived and one soon emerges at the 'col' between Carnedd Lŵyd (616m.) on your right and Cadair Idris (893m.) on your left. Continue running along the Pony Path as it gently rises towards the rim of Cadair Idris. As one approaches the top, the views down the steep cliffs towards Llyn y Gadair (**GR 718136**) are spectacular!

Continue running on the narrow, rocky path as it ascends to the trig point at the summit. This section can become quite crowded with walkers so please take care here. At the top you have a choice. One can either return to the valley by the same way or, continue running over the summit rocks in a north easterly direction until a narrow path begins to traverse across the top of an open scree gully (**GR 713133**). From here descend the steep scree slope with care, zig-zagging your way trying to find the most stable sections! Again, be aware of others, especially people below you, with regard to loose rocks and stones etc.

4. At the base of the scree slope you will arrive at the picturesque Llyn y Gadair. Again, you have two choices here. You can either, take the foot-path that descends in a northerly direction, passing Llyn Gafr (**GR 710141**) and arriving opposite the Gwernan Lake Hotel or, from

The steep scree descent takes a line left of the snow field & follows a zigzag route down the centre of the spur.

Llyn y Gadair take a less-defined path over moorland (boggy in places) and rocks that re-joins the Pony Path at GR 696143. From here, continue to retrace your steps to Ty Nant and the National Trust car park.

NANTLLE RIDGE CIRCUIT
ROUTE 14

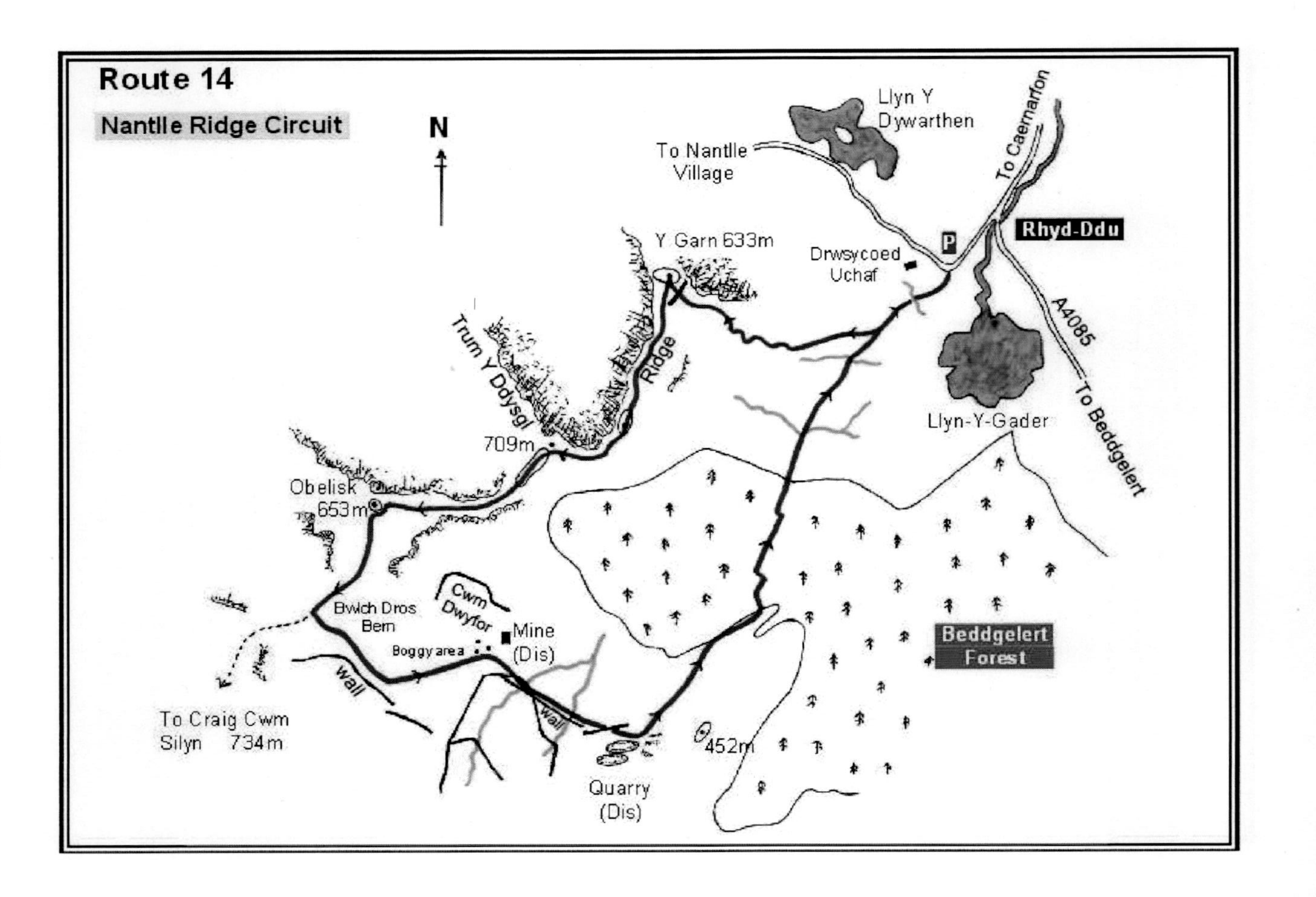

Route 14
Nantlle Ridge Circuit
N
Llyn Y Dywarthen
To Nantlle Village
To Caernarfon
Rhyd-Ddu
P
Y Garn 633m
Drwsycoed Uchaf
A4085
To Beddgelert
Trum Y Ddysgl
Ridge
Llyn-Y-Gader
709m
Obelisk 653m
Cwm Dwyfor
Bwlch Dros Bern
Mine (Dis)
Boggy area
Beddgelert Forest
wall
wall
To Craig Cwm Silyn 734m
452m
Quarry (Dis)

ROUTE 14: NANTLLE RIDGE CIRCUIT

DISTANCE: 6.5 Miles
ASCENT: Min. 204 metres @ start. Max. 709 metres.
TERRAIN: Situated in the shadow of the Snowdon Group of mountains, the superb Nantlle Ridge Circuit consists of long grassy ridge slopes and cwms with intervals of steep rocky sections and easy scrambling. Some of these cwms are quite boggy so pack spare socks and a towel for afterwards! This superb ridge run includes several summits along the way with excellent views and positions throughout. It is also a popular walking route so expect to hear the 'one size fits all' tapping of walking poles around you! Although not as serious as maybe some of its Snowdon counterparts, do not underestimate this run. Being one of the more 'remote' areas, it is advisable to carry full running kit and refreshments etc.
TIME: 2 – 2 ½ Hours depending on navigation and stops.
START: Roadside lay-by on B4418 slightly south west of Rhyd Ddu village at GR 567526 (shared with Route 9, 'Mynydd Mawr').
O.S MAP: 1:25,000 Sheet North Wales OL17.
GRADIENT: Very steep initial ascent followed by easy scrambling sections. The descent slopes can become quite water-logged in places and are difficult to avoid.
ACCESS: No known access issues or restrictions on this route.

Grid References

552526	Summit cairn at 633m
548518	'Mynydd Drws-y-Coed'
545516	'Trum y Ddysgl'
535514	'Mynydd-y-Mignedd'
532507	'Bwlch Dros Bern'
536504	Slope eases and broadens
542505	Copper mine below 'Cwm Dwyfor'
550500	Old slate quarry (Dis)
554556	Beddgelert Forest
557513	Small stream and bridge
558517	Stream crossing

FGS Grading: Grading is: F13 [D2, N3, T2, R3, H3]

Distance	**2**	6 – 12 Miles
Navigation	**3**	Expert navigation skills needed.
Terrain	**2**	25 – 50% on graded track or path 50 -75% off track.
Remoteness	**3**	Remote, isolated location.
Height	**3**	Over 250 ft per mile.

Route Description :

1. From the parking space, locate the obvious footpath that runs across farmland, passing over a small bridge. The path now becomes alarmingly steep as it ascends the narrow, broken path up 'Y Garn'. This slope is a 'killer' and a thigh pump is guaranteed! However, this is the most sustained uphill section so you can keep telling yourself "It's easy after this!"... Don't let me fool you! Around the 600m contour, it begins to ease slightly and then passes over a ladder stile in a wall. Awkward boulders and rocks (care here!) have to be negotiated in order to reach the summit cairn at 633m, **GR 552526**.

Running across the initial farmland section.
Photo by Julia Kelly.

2. Now run along the broad ridge southwards and ascend the narrow, rocky ridge above 'Clogwyn Marchnad'. This is easier than it looks with several delightful scrambling sections in an exposed setting. Continue along this to the summit of the next peak, 'Mynydd Drws-y-Coed' (695m), **GR 548518**. Run along the narrow ridge as it swings westerly towards the flat top of 'Trum y Ddysgl', the highest point on this run at 709m (**GR 545516**).

About to tackle the very steep climb to the summit of Y Garn.
Photo by Julia Kelly.

3. Now descend the grassy hill slope south west, veering to the right and running along the narrow rocky path up towards the 'Obelisk (!)' on 'Mynydd-y-Mignedd' at 653m (**GR 535514**). From the Obelisk, head in a southerly direction to the 'col' below, marked as 'Bwlch Dros Bern', 516m and at **GR 532507**. At the col, descend the steep, grassy slope in a south easterly direction, heading towards a wall and stream marked as 'Ceunant yr Allt' on the O.S.map. There are no real land marks or paths to look out for here so use of the map is essential. At **GR 536504**, the slope eases and broadens out somewhat. Now head due east in the direction of the old copper mine below 'Cwm Dwyfor' at **GR 542505**. This whole section from the col can be quite boggy underfoot in many parts. It is doubtful that you will reach the mine with dry feet! (unless in the middle of a drought!)

4. At the mine workings, head south for a short distance and locate the long, broken drystone wall that traverses the hillside in a south easterly direction towards an old slate quarry (Dis) at **GR 550500**. This wall has a vague, broken path running alongside it, passing through wet sections where two small streams cross it.

5. At the slate quarry, the track becomes better defined and this is run gently uphill in a north easterly direction, ending up at the fringe of the pine trees in Beddgelert Forest. At **GR 554556**., the forest is entered. The rough path soon connects with a forestry road which carries on in a north easterly direction, passing over a small stream and bridge at **GR 557513**. After a few metres, turn left through the pine trees and locate a rough, stony path towards the base of the eastern slopes of Mynydd Drws y Coed and Y Garn. Another stream is crossed at **GR 558517**. This section too can become quite wet and muddy, especially after heavy rain. However, from here you can view your parked up car in the distance, safe in the knowledge that in a few minutes a dry towel, dry socks and clean, dry trainers await!

NOTE: *There is scope* ***to 'extend'*** *this route beyond the col at Bwlch Dros Barn by running to the summit of 'Craig Cwm Silyn' (734m) and then on to Carnedd Goch Trig. Point (700m). From Carnedd Coch, descend the grass slope in a north westerly direction towards a gate in the transverse drystone wall (**GR 504503**). Follow the public footpath to the top end of the minor road at **GR 496511**. However, in order to complete this 'variation', a second car is required to be parked up at this point! Otherwise a very long, tiring road section back to Rhyd Ddu in fell running shoes is the option. Hmmm? Now let me think……!?*

MOEL HEBOG CIRCUIT
ROUTE 15

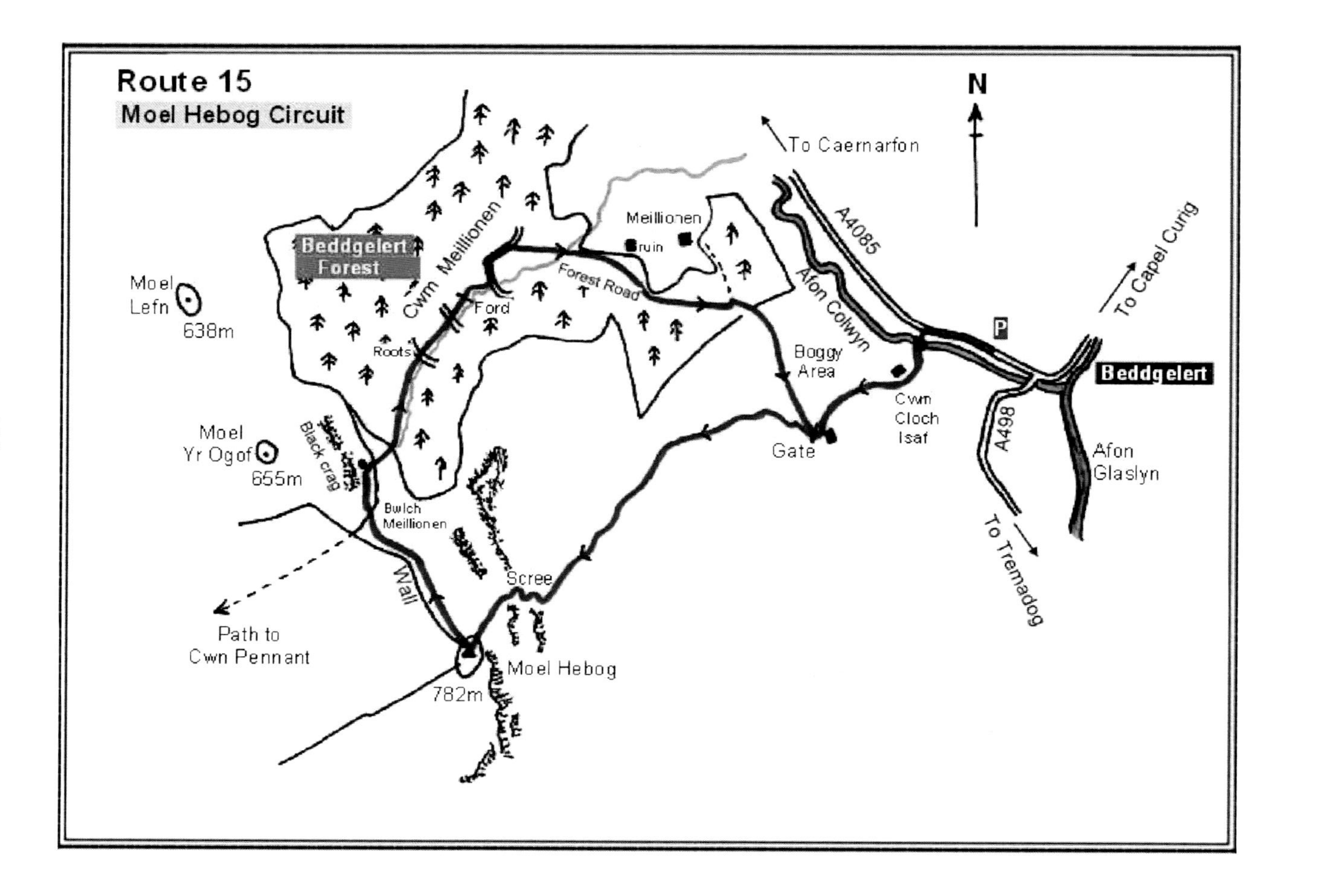
Route 15
Moel Hebog Circuit
N
To Caernarfon
A4085
Afon Colwyn
P
To Capel Curig
Beddgelert
Afon Glaslyn
A498
To Tremadog
Cwn Cloch Isaf
Boggy Area
Gate
Meillionen
ruin
Forest Road
Ford
Cwm Meillionen
Beddgelert Forest
Roots
Moel Lefn
638m
Moel Yr Ogof
655m
Black crag
Bwlch Meillionen
Wall
Scree
Path to Cwn Pennant
Moel Hebog
782m

ROUTE 15: MOEL HEBOG CIRCUIT

DISTANCE: 6 Miles
ASCENT: Min.60 metres @ start.Max.782 metres.
TERRAIN: This superb mountain route has to be a 'must' for any visiting runner(s) to this area. Moel Hebog dominates the skyline above the tourist town of Beddgelert. With a varied combination of challenging running surfaces and brilliant situations, this run maintains interest throughout. On a clear day, the 360 degree summit views across Snowdonia must rank as some of the best anywhere to be found in the region! However, as with all high mountain routes, it should never be underestimated. This is a remote area and not the location to twist an ankle or get into difficulty. The first half of the run involves loose rocks and scree in the upper sections. In contrast, the descent through Beddgelert Forest follows a narrow path with is not only boggy in places but also has many exposed and slippery tree roots. Care should be exercised here!
TIME: 1¾ - 2¼ depending on navigation/photo stops.
START: Beddgelert Village, car park at GR 587483, just off the main A4085.
O.S MAP: 1:25,000 Sheet North Wales OL17.
GRADIENT: Steep, sustained climbs and descents throughout the route.
ACCESS: No known access issues.

Grid References

587483	Car park starting/ finishing point
585483	Left turn onto public footpath/ tarmac road
568472	Rocky terraces
560475	Junction of paths at Bwlch Meillionen
562478	Wooden stile over forestry fence
566486	Left turn onto a forestry track
572488	'Beudy Ysgubor'
577485	Footpath leading to stream
581479	Farm house
575488	'Meillionen'

FGS Grading: Grading is: F10 [D1, N2, T2, R2, H3]

Distance	**1**	6 - 12 miles
Navigation	**2**	Competent navigation skills needed.
Terrain	**2**	25 – 50% on graded track or path 50 - 75% off track.
Remoteness	**2**	Countryside not in close proximity to habitation – less than 20% of the route within 2 miles.
Height	**3**	Over 250 ft per mile.

Approaching the summit cairn and Trig Point at the top of Moel Hebog.
Photo by Julia Kelly.

Route Description :

1. Park in the free car park just off the A 4085 near to the 'Gelert' Outdoor Store (**GR 588483**). Run up the main road, passing the 'Gelert' shop on your left, towards a public footpath that turns left over a bridge crossing the Afon Colwyn (**GR 585483**). Run along this 'private road' passing under a railway bridge and over two other narrow-gauge railway tracks. Continue up the tarmac road as far as a farmhouse on your left. Take the rising footpath ahead of you, accessed via a gate in the wall and follow it across rough grassland.

Running up the pleasant, easy angled grassland section with Cnicht in the far distance. Photo by Julia Kelly.

2. At this point, Hebog looms high above you in the far distance. Gently angled at first, it does not take long for the path to become a steeper proposition. It also becomes more rocky as it leaves the valley slopes far below. A series of 'cairns' marks the route as one has to negotiate rocky steps and clefts.

The grassy shoulder above the scree path.
Photo by Juila Kelly.

Eventually, you will arrive at the base of a rocky slope forming a series of 'terraces' at **GR 568472**. These terraces are linked via a steep scree path that wends its way left and right, avoiding the rocky outcrops direct. The top of Hebog now appears very close. The scree path soon eases and one ends up at a grassy shoulder where the views of Snowdonia are truly exceptional.

3. At this point, Moel yr Ogof lies below you in a northerly direction (**GR 556479**). It is worth spending a moment or two getting your bearings and locating your line of descent. A short run in a southerly direction, via some rocks, leads to the summit cairn and Trig Point at the top of Moel Hebog at 782m.

4. If it is clear, stop for a few moments and 'soak up' the view.... You may even use this opportunity to size up your next route! From the summit locate the very obvious drystone wall that descends from the cairn, in a north westerly direction, all the way to the 'col' between Hebog and Moel yr Ogof. The descent slope delightfully consists of short grass with surface stones lower down. At **GR 560475** another footpath is met at an area named 'Bwlch Meillionen'. Turn right and follow this alongside another wall in a northerly direction. This can get a touch slippery over some of the exposed rocks so take care here. High above you on your left is a huge black crag draped in moss and other hanging plants. It's all a bit 'Jurassic Park' here! As you descend you will arrive at a large rectangular boulder with a tree growing out of its top. Just after this cut right and down to a forestry fence where a wooden stile (**GR 562478**) allows access to the area known as Beddgelert Forest. Locating this stile can be tricky. Do not be tempted to follow the path beyond the large boulder. If you start going uphill again you have gone too far!

5. At the stile cross it and follow the narrow forest path downhill, marked by a small 'post'. The path follows the course of a small stream and, as a result, it is boggy in places. Expect to get wet feet here in all but the driest conditions. There are also many slippery, exposed roots from where tree felling has taken place. However, the path improves as one descends, passing over several forestry roads. At **GR 566486** turn left onto a forestry track and run along it a short distance until a marker post points the way of the path once again. Here it runs through some dense trees to emerge at another track with three ways on. Turn right and stay on the wide forestry road as it descends in an easterly direction towards 'Beudy Ysgubor', an old ruined barn (**GR 572488**).

6. Continue to run on this track, descending gently all the way to a left turn hairpin bend, in an area marked as 'Parc Ty' n-y Coed'. Just after the hairpin, a sign points to a footpath on the right which passes through more trees and fords a stream (**GR 577485**). Run along this reasonably defined path, negotiating some wet, marshy sections, towards the farmhouse where you originally started to run uphill to Moel Hebog (**GR 581479**). Go through the gate, turn left and retrace the initial section back to the car park in Beddgelert.

Beddgelert Forest stretching out in front of you. The descent follows the vague clearing in the centre of the picture. Photo by Julia Kelly.

Variations and extensions exist for this route, the obvious one being to continue up Moel yr Ogof, over to Moel Lefn and down to the head of Cwm Pennant where a path leads through Beddgelert Forest in an easterly direction, connecting with another path leading to 'Meillionen' at GR 575488. From here, the path continues to the hairpin at Parc Ty' n-Coed and finishes as for Route 15. Whatever you choose, you are guaranteed to have a great run and one which you will, hopefully, return to again in the future.

MOEL SIABOD
ROUTE 16

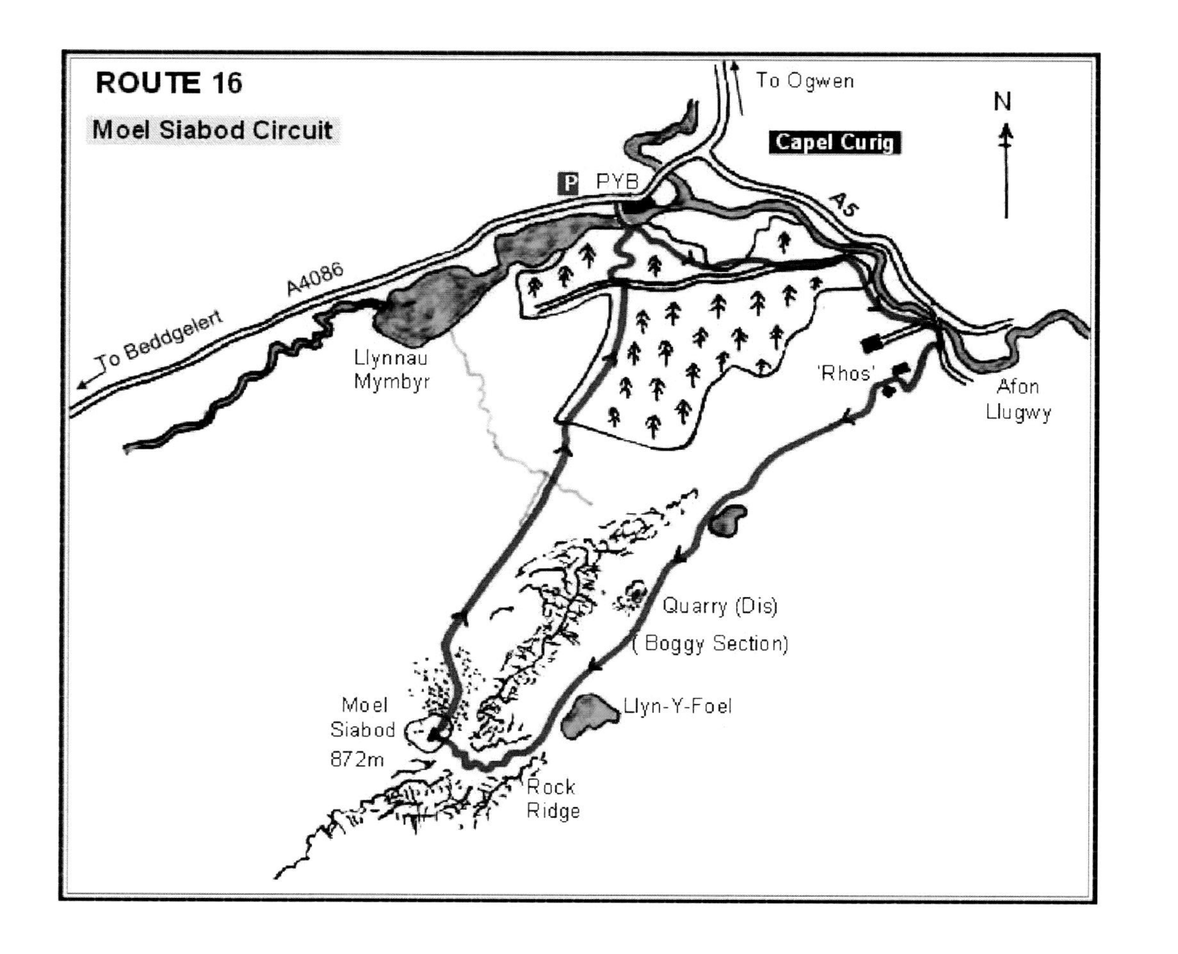

ROUTE 16
Moel Siabod Circuit
To Ogwen
N
Capel Curig
P
PYB
A5
A4086
To Beddgelert
Llynnau Mymbyr
'Rhos'
Afon Llugwy
Quarry (Dis)
(Boggy Section)
Llyn-Y-Foel
Moel Siabod 872m
Rock Ridge

ROUTE 16: MOEL SIABOD

DISTANCE: 7.5 Miles.
ASCENT: Min.195 metres @ start. Max. 872 metres.
TERRAIN: Moel Siabod (pronounced 'Sha-bod') is the first large mountain one sees when entering Snowdonia via the A5, passing through the village of Capel Curig. It is a bit like a mountain of two halves. On the north west side it appears as a smooth, rounded grassy slope with some rocky bits at its summit. However from the southern side, it consists of a steep rocky summit ridge bounded by a huge, steep face split by several large, scree-covered gullies. As a result, this run is extremely varied with regard to the terrain covered. Owing to its remote location and height it should not be underestimated, especially in poor weather conditions. Full running safety kit should be carried.
TIME: 2 ½ hours depending on stops and weather conditions.
START: Roadside parking just west of Plas y Brenin.
O.S MAP: 1:25,000 Sheet North Wales OL17/ OL18 (please note this route is split across two map sheets. However, the full route can be found on the 1:50,000 sheet no.115)
GRADIENT: Continually climbing with some very steep sections on the rock ridge leading to the summit.
ACCESS: No known access issues. However, please do not park on Plas y Brenin property and respect footpath requests by land owners.

Grid References

715578	Roadside parking on the A4086 near Plas y Brenin.
731575	Path descends to Afon Llugwy.
717555	Disused slate quarry.
712546	Start of the rock ridge to Moel Siabod summit.
715547	Moel Siabod summit @ 872m.
712562	Wet, boggy section on descent.
716577	Plas y Brenin footbridge.

FGS Grading: F11 [D1, N2, T2, R3, H3]

Distance	**1**	6 - 12 miles
Navigation	**2**	Competent navigation skills needed.
Terrain	**2**	25 – 50% on graded track or path 50 - 75% off track.
Remoteness	**3**	Remote isolated location.
Height	**3**	Over 250ft per mile.

The author Jim Kelly roughly half way on the ascent of the rock ridge. Photo by Julia Kelly.

Route Description :

The route detailed here is described as a circuit, taking in both sides of the mountain. However, it is possible to run this as a straight up and down route beginning in the village of Capel Curig and tackling Siabod on its northern side via the forestry plantation above Plas y Brenin outdoor centre. It is also possible to run the circuit either clockwise or anti-clockwise. This decision will depend on whether, as a runner or runners, you prefer to either ascend or descend the long, scrambly rock ridge on the southern side. **The description here is 'clockwise', using the rock ridge as a means of ascent.**

1. For either direction, park and start at the roadside lay-by just west of Plas y Brenin on the A4086. (Do not park on the official PYB parking areas!) Run towards PYB and take the descending footpath signposted 'Moel Siabod' over a wooden footbridge. Instead of heading straight up (the route of the anti-clockwise option), take a left turn just after the footbridge and follow a good gravel vehicle track and path eastwards all the way to Capel Curig. At **GR 731575**, the path narrows and drops down to the edge of the Afon Llugwy, and continues across fields to join a minor, tarmac road. At the minor road turn right and follow it uphill until signs direct you onto a public footpath. Please be aware that the owners of the farm, marked 'Rhos' on the map, have diverted the general public away from their property. Please follow and obey signage.

2. Proceed upwards along the footpath which soon joins a better farm track leading towards a lake with a low dam and some old slate quarries at **GR 717555**. On your right hand side you will now be under the large, rocky south eastern face of Moel Siabod. You will also soon be in full view of the rocky ridge which has to be ascended in order to reach the top.

On the approach to the rock ridge leading to the summit of Moel Siabod at 872 metres. Llyn Y Foel is on the left of this photo. Photo by Julia Kelly.

This is a very pleasant section up and over steps, blocks and boulders. The views and positions during this ascent (weather permitting!) are outstanding! Be aware that the grassy section before the ridge can become quite boggy. Alas, be prepared for wet feet here. Unless, of course, you are one of those ingenious runners who will try to create a dry way at all costs, even if it means deviating via the 'Azores'!!

3. The rock ridge (**GR 712546**) leads all the way, steeply, to the summit trig point and cairn/rock shelter at 872m (**GR 715547**). On a clear day, a 360 degree view of Snowdonia awaits the runner, which is simply spectacular. The route now, by contrast, goes across boulders at first, to the path descending the well-formed, long grassy slope, all the way back to Plas y Brenin. One or two wet, boggy sections are encountered at **GR 712562** where the path follows a small stream in its descent.

At **GR 713565** a stile and fence are met. Go over this and continue down the narrow, sometimes rocky path to the forestry plantation below.

On the descent toward Plas Y Brenin and the lakes of Llynnau, Mymbyr
Photo by Julia Kelly.

4. The run now descends pleasantly through the huge pine trees.
At **GR 715574**, a wide forestry track is met. Turn left here and, after a few metres, turn immediately right, descending another narrow path through the trees.

5. At **GR 716577** one reaches the Plas y Brenin footbridge over the lake outflow. Go across this, up the path and your vehicle awaits you.

INTERNATIONAL SNOWDON RACE ROUTE
ROUTE 17

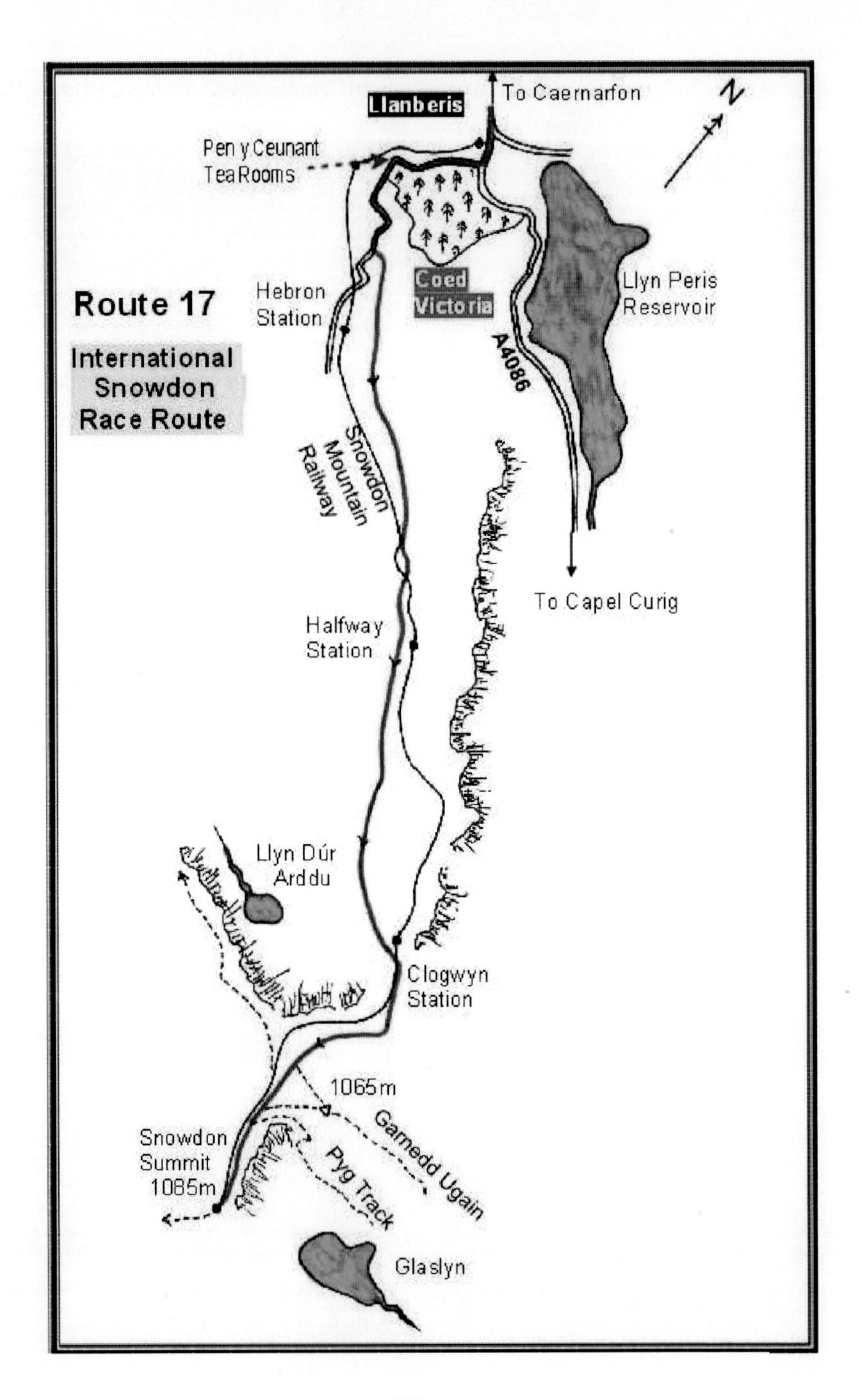
Llanberis
To Caernarfon
N
Pen y Ceunant
Tea Rooms
Coed
Victoria
Llyn Peris
Reservoir
Route 17
International
Snowdon
Race Route
Hebron
Station
A4086
Snowdon
Mountain
Railway
To Capel Curig
Halfway
Station
Llyn Dúr
Arddu
Clogwyn
Station
1065m
Garnedd Ugain
Snowdon
Summit
1085m
Pyg Track
Glaslyn

ROUTE 17: INTERNATIONAL SNOWDON RACE ROUTE (Llanberis Path)

DISTANCE: 10 Miles
ASCENT: Min.105 metres @ start.1085 Max. metres.
TERRAIN: This is basically a fast "up and down" route taking the line of the International Snowdon Race from the village of Llanberis to Snowdon summit. It is run entirely on an engineered rocky path that is sustained uphill with some steep sections in its latter half. In winter this can ice up considerably. Indeed, as this route runs up Wales' highest peak, it should not be underestimated, particularly in doubtful weather or in the winter months. Don't become an MRT 'statistic!'
TIME: Average 1hr 40' to 2hrs + (Record of 1hr 02' 29" in 1985!)
START: Park at G.R. 576606 opposite 'Coed y Glyn' or, any one of the pay & display car parks in the village.
O.S MAP: 1:25,000 Sheet North Wales OL17.
GRADIENT: This route is sustained uphill with some steep sections. Fast, hard descent... watch your knees and don't trip!
ACCESS: The run is entirely on a busy public footpath, especially during the spring and summer months. No access issues. However, please bear in mind this is a very popular route with tourists and walkers. Please try to avoid knocking them over, especially on your rapid descent!

Grid References

576606	Car parking in Llanberis.
584597	Mini roundabout
607548	Convergence of Crib Goch/ Miners' Track paths.

FGS Grading: Grading is F7 [D1, N1, T0, R2, H3]

Distance	1	6 -12 miles
Navigation	1	Basic navigation skills needed
Terrain	0	75% + on graded track or path
Remoteness	2	Countryside not in close proximity to habitation – less than 20% of the route within 2 miles
Height	3	Over 250ft per mile

Route Description :

1. Run through Llanberis Village passing the Snowdon Mountain Railway Station on your right and up towards the Royal Victoria Hotel on the left. At the mini roundabout **GR 584597**, turn right in to Victoria Terrace. (Alternative route here is to run a little further on from the mini roundabout and take a rising footpath through the woods marked as 'Coed Victoria'.)

Back at Victoria Terrace, follow the road, flat at first, to a cattle grid. From here, say goodbye to the horizontal because, now the route begins to climb all the way to Snowdon Summit! Continue up the twisting minor road passing Pen y Ceunant Tea Rooms (remember this on your descent... log fire, fresh coffee and great cakes... put a fiver in your running shorts!) until you reach a track clearly marked on the left marked 'Cader Ellyll' on the map. This is known as the 'Llanberis Path' to the top of Snowdon and is the easiest, if not the shortest, way to the summit at 1085m. The track is extremely well defined and has been built to cater for the 1,000's of tourists and walkers that at least decide to take the calorie-burning trek to the top rather than opt for the expensive 'couch potato express!'

2. The track runs basically parallel to the train and climbs steadily to point **GR 604563** where the gradient suddenly increases. From the 630m contour to the 950m contour you have to dig deep and push those quads! At 950m there's a brief respite where the track flattens somewhat. At 998m (**GR 607548**) you may experience an increase in other people on the mountain. This is the point at which the routes Crib Goch and the Miner's Track converge before leading to the summit. The angle now increases once more as one has to slalom and weave their way around the walkers and tourists shuffling their way to the summit. On reaching the top, with the new Hafod Eryri Café and train Station, you know what to do!

3. Yes, that's right... turn round and 'gas it' back down to Llanberis as fast as you can. However, on a serious note, please be aware of others around you. Whatever one's opinions on Snowdon as a 'tourist attraction', they have as much right as anyone else to be there. Let us not give runners a bad name!

4. Either complete your run in Llanberis or, remember that fiver in your shorts and take ½ hour out for that coffee at the tea rooms to reflect the fact that the men's record for this run is 1.02.29 set in 1985. The women's record of 1.12.48 was set in 1995. At the time of writing this guide, both records still stand! A sobering thought!

Kenny Stuart on his record breaking Snowdon race in 1985 in 1:02:29.
So far, this has not been beaten.
Photo : Kenny Stuart archive Collection.

SNOWDON HORSEHOE
ROUTE 18

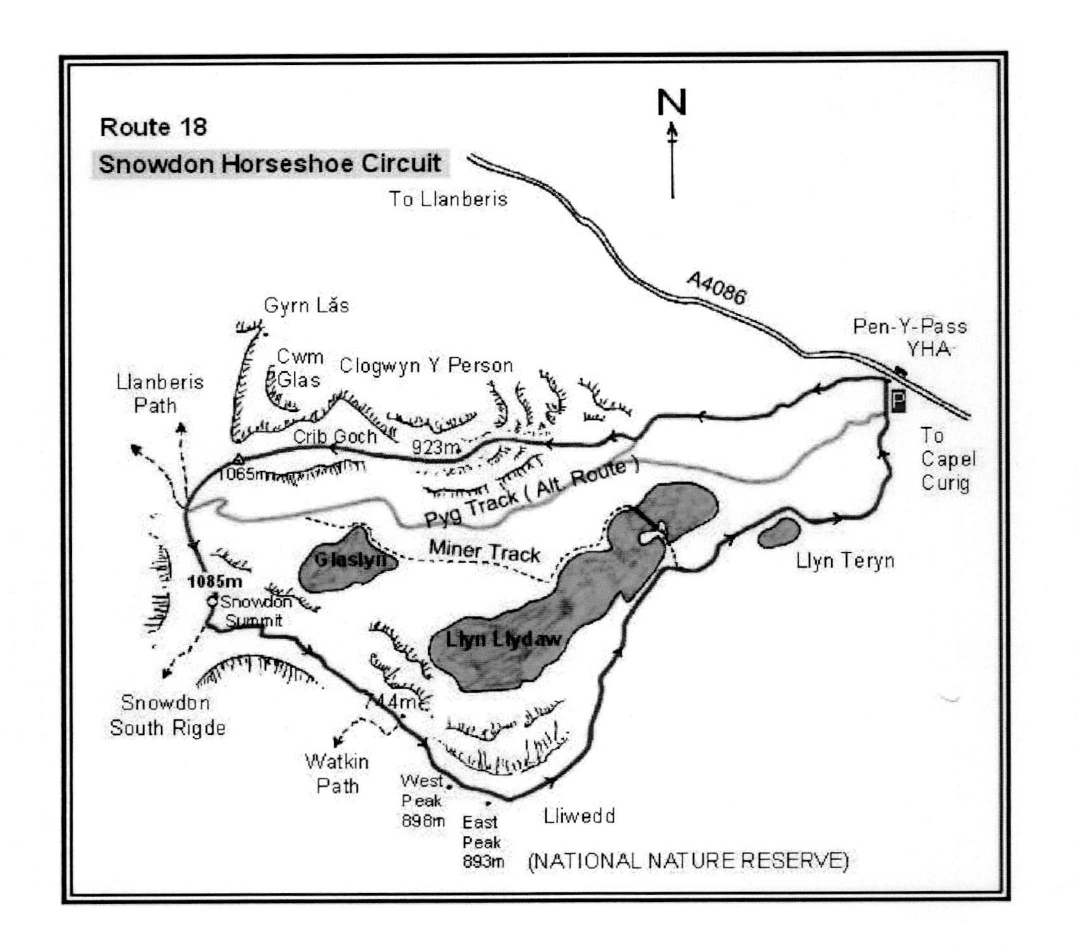

Route 18
Snowdon Horseshoe Circuit
N
To Llanberis
A4086
Pen-Y-Pass
YHA
P
To
Capel
Curig
Gyrn Lăs
Cwm
Glas
Clogwyn Y Person
Llanberis
Path
Crib Goch
923m
1065m
Pyg Track (Alt. Route)
Miner Track
Glaslyn
Llyn Teryn
1085m
Snowdon
Summit
Llyn Llydaw
744m
Snowdon
South Rigde
Watkin
Path
West
Peak
898m
East
Peak
893m
Lliwedd
(NATIONAL NATURE RESERVE)

ROUTE 18: SNOWDON HORSESHOE

DISTANCE: 7 Miles from Pen y Pass Car Park. 9.6 miles if 'alternative start' is used from Pont y Cromlech on the Llanberis Pass.
ASCENT: Min.359 *(208m Pont y Cromlech)* metres @ start .Max.1085 Metres, Snowdon Summit.
TERRAIN: Falling into the 'mountain' category, this run is about as good as it gets! Continually sustained over steep rocky ground, it requires the runner to demonstrate a good level of off-road running techniques and fitness. The terrain is a cocktail of steep rocky paths, loose scree, high rocky pinnacles, steps and ridges with a short section on a good gravel track. Being amongst the highest peaks in the UK, Snowdon should never be underestimated. Despite its 'marketing' as a tourist attraction, regrettably, it claims several lives each year, often through personal negligence and/or inexperience. Please be aware that this route is inadvisable in strong winds or adverse weather conditions. In the event of being 'caught out' whilst on Crib Goch then an emergency descent can be made north west from Bwlch Coch (GR 622552) towards Llyn Glas, or south towards Glaslyn (GR 616545). If bad weather approaches whilst on Snowdon, consider 'bailing out' by descending via the 'Pyg or Miners' Track.
TIME: 3 - 3 ½ hours average (depending on stops).
START: Pen y Pass YHA/ Car park, GR 647556. Alternatively, at the time of going to press, you can park for 'free' at Pont y Cromlech lay-by GR 630565. This adds a further 2.6 miles to the total distance.
O.S MAP: 1:25,000 Sheet North Wales OL17.
GRADIENT: Continually steep and sustained with 'Grade 1' rock scrambling sections on Crib Goch and Lliwedd. Steep descents off Snowdon via the North Ridge 'Watkin Path' and dropping down off Lliwedd on the return to Pen y Pass.
ACCESS: No access issues. However, the area around Lliwedd is designated a National Nature Reserve. Please obey the by-laws affecting this.

Grid References

647556	Pen y Pass car park/ YHA
630565	Pont y Cromlech alternative start
634553	Bwlch y Moch
611552	Trig point at Crib y Ddysgl
609543	Rock spike
619537	Bwlch Ciliau
635544	Cwm Dyli

FGS Grading: Grading is F12 [D1, N2, T3, R3, H3]

Distance	1	6 -12 miles
Navigation	2	Competent navigation skills needed.
Terrain	3	Under 25% on graded track or path. Over 75% off track.
Remoteness	3	Remote, isolated location.
Height	3	Over 250 ft per mile

The spectacular vista of Snowdon (Yr Wyddfa) & the lake of Glaslyn dominates this route.

Route Description :

This is probably the most dramatic, exposed mountain run in Snowdonia and, of course, the highest route in Wales (and England for that matter!). It should only be attempted by experienced mountain runners comfortable on high mountain terrain. Indeed, sections of it fall within the 'rock scrambling' category, albeit at a low grade. However, it is a run where a steady head is required on certain sections. For those not used to traversing exposed, high, narrow, knife-edged ridge terrain, then either take it very steady or, opt for one of the two lower-level paths which avoid Crib Goch entirely with hardly any difference in distance.

Assuming you are brave and opting for the Crib Goch variation, please bear in mind that you will encounter many other walkers/ scramblers on this ridge. Please give anyone the time they need to traverse the difficult sections and show courtesy. If you are travelling faster than others, they will 'give way' to you whenever it is possible and safe to do so.
For this run, please make sure that you carry full mountain running kit, i.e. drink (at least 1Ltr.), compass, whistle, waterproof running top, hat, gloves, emergency snack and a camera.. the setting is truly stunning! In summer, head band, sunglasses and sun bloc are advised.

Although it is possible to run the Horseshoe in a clockwise direction, most visitors tackle it 'anti-clockwise'. I guess this due to the satisfaction gained from climbing up the superb east ridge of Crib Goch and the breathtaking vista of the whole route that is continually in front of you, rather than behind.

Two starting points are suggested for this run, on account of the ever increasing pay & display charges at Pen y Pass car park (currently £10 at the time of going to press!). For the wealthy amongst us or, car full of 4 persons sharing the cost, the charges at the Pen y Pass start are probably no real issue. However, an alternative is to begin at the 'free' lay-by at Pont y Cromlech. This adds approximately 2.6 miles in total to the route. **However, one thing both car parking areas have in common is that, by 9.30 am, on most days, especially at weekends, both are usually full! The 'greener' alternative is to locate the 'Park & Ride' bus service that operates out of Nant Peris to Pen y Pass and use that instead. Details of which can be found through Llanberis T.I.O.**

1. From Pen y Pass car park, run along the Pyg Track as far as **GR 634553**, marked on the OS Map as 'Bwlch y Moch'.

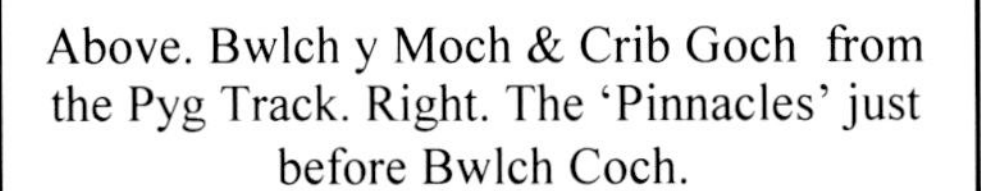

Above. Bwlch y Moch & Crib Goch from the Pyg Track. Right. The 'Pinnacles' just before Bwlch Coch.

Here, that path splits and Crib Goch is clearly signposted. It is on this early section of the run that you will encounter the majority of walking parties setting out on their "day ont' hills!" However, once you take the rather loose, rocky route towards Crib Goch, which looms above you at this point, the casual walking crowds tend to thin out as they continue their ascent via the continuation of the Pyg Track. Crib Goch now rises steeply and soon one has to resort to simple scrambling techniques in order to make upward progress. A series of short, rocky steps are taken in a magnificent setting! The route is 'well worn' so follow the polished hand and footholds to a point on the ridge where you emerge on to some angular, reddish-brown rock. Follow this rocky crest until you reach its top where it flattens. In front of you now lies the excellent Crib Goch Ridge which is traversed on its left-hand side. Tackle this section carefully, using the top of the ridge for handholds and a series of large polished holds for your feet. Carry on past Bwlch Coch where some more, but easier, scrambling leads you to Crib y Ddysgl and the trig point at 1065m.(**GR 611552**) From here, the route joins the 'Llanberis Path' (see Route 17) as it climbs its way up rocky steps to the summit cairn and café at 1085m.

The view from Snowdon Summit (1085m) looking south westerly towards the 'new' Hafod Eryri summit café and Station with a more 'picturesque' Tremadog Bay in the far distance.

2. Once at the top, immediately descend in a south westerly direction to **GR 609543** and locate a rock 'spike' that denotes the beginning of your loose, stony descent down this section of the, so-called, 'Watkin Path'. Eventually, this levels out at around the 750m contour and continues like this until you arrive at Bwlch Ciliau (**GR619537**). Instead of heading down, continue straight ahead and upwards towards Lliwedd's West Peak at 898m. More easy scrambling punctuates the vague stony path that you follow here. It's worth noting here that the views across the Horseshoe are truly magnificent. The 900 foot drop down Lliwedd's North Face is impressive too.You will be relieved to know that once you have crossed Lliwedd's East Peak at 893m, all the uphill difficulties are over. Continue running along the stony path as it descends, steep in places, towards Cwm Dyli (**GR 635544**) and Llyn Llydaw Reservoir. One's legs will be tired at this stage so take care with footing and speed and avoid any nasty trips!

3. Eventually, the world of the horizontal is met as one joins the Miner's Track. Turn right here and head along this gravel track down towards Pen y Pass, whizzing once again, past hordes of walkers and 'casual tourists' who will probably look at you in such a way as to imply that "you must be mad or need your head testing!" Oddly enough, when you take a cursory glance at their 'town shoes and Chinos' one really has to smile internally and consider the irony you have just witnessed!

Incidentally, congratulations… you have just completed one of the best mountain runs in the UK! Well done you!

The dark north-facing mass of Lliwedd rises ahead of you as run towards Bwlch Ciliau.

PERIS HORSESHOE CIRCUIT
ROUTE 19

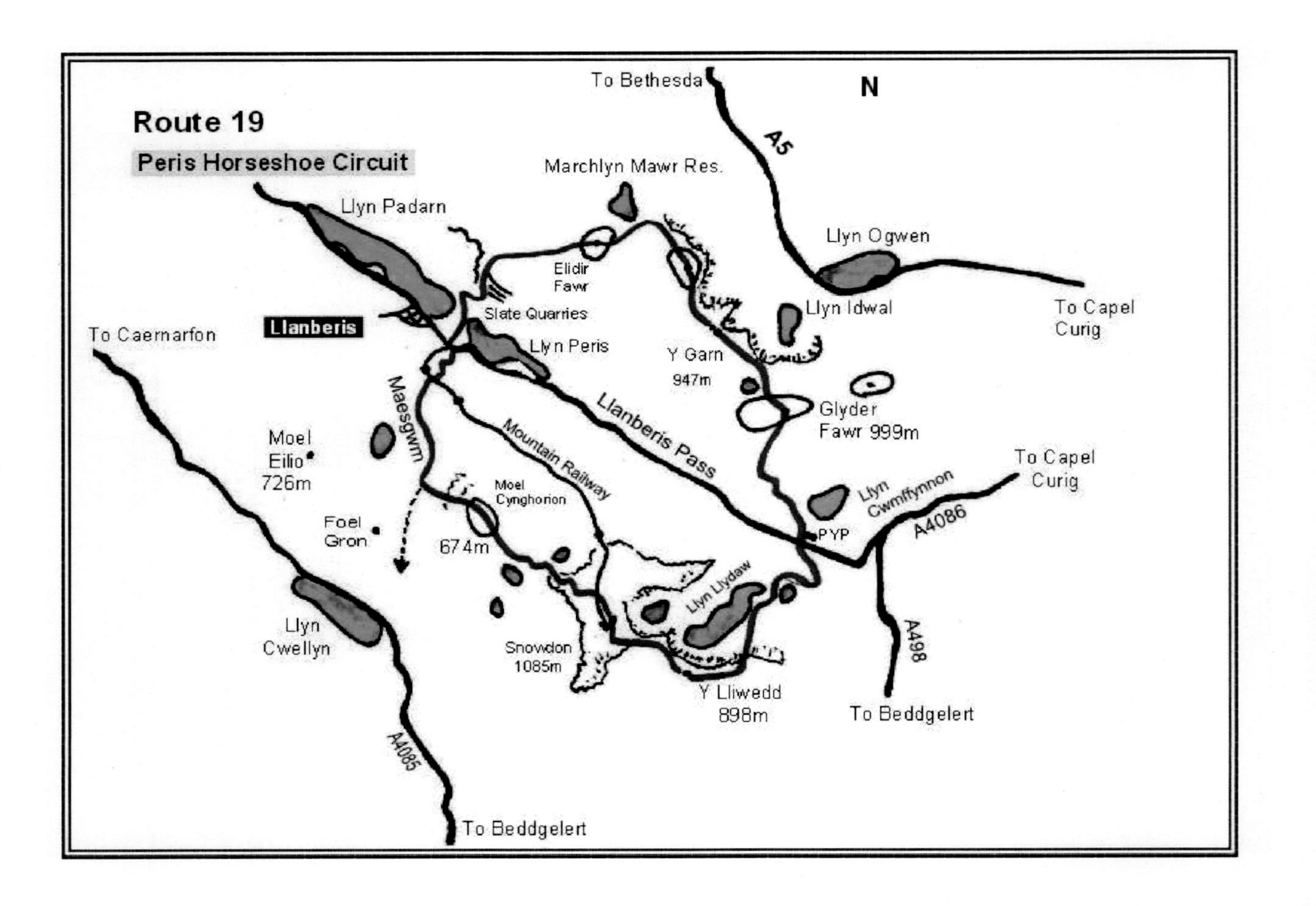

Route 19
Peris Horseshoe Circuit
To Bethesda
N
A5
Marchlyn Mawr Res.
Llyn Padarn
Llyn Ogwen
Elidir Fawr
Slate Quarries
Llanberis
Llyn Idwal
To Capel Curig
To Caernarfon
Llyn Peris
Y Garn
947m
Maesgwm
Llanberis Pass
Glyder Fawr 999m
Moel Eilio
726m
Mountain Railway
To Capel Curig
Moel Cynghorion
Llyn Cwmffynnon
A4086
Foel Gron
674m
PYP
Llyn Llydaw
A498
Llyn Cwellyn
Snowdon 1085m
Y Lliwedd 898m
To Beddgelert
A4085
To Beddgelert

ROUTE 19: PERIS HORSESHOE CIRCUIT

DISTANCE: 17.5 Miles
ASCENT: Min.105 metres @ start. Max.1085 metres. (Total ascent on this route: 8,500 ft!)
TERRAIN: This is a physically demanding route of the highest calibre. It requires considerable levels of stamina, fitness and high mountain running ability. The run involves some very steep terrain in both ascent and descent covering a variety of rock and slope types, all in a very remote setting. It would be totally inadvisable to attempt this route in bad or uncertain weather conditions. For this run you will require a hydration pack with 1 – 1.5L capacity, map, compass, whistle, mobile phone, waterproof top and trousers, hat, gloves, emergency snacks/ 'gels' and take some money. Please note that the Snowdon Summit Café/ Station closes during the late Autumn and Winter months! Each September, the 'Peris Horseshoe Fell Race', organised by Mike Blake of the ERYRI Harriers, is often used as a 'warm up' to the Snowdonia Marathon at the end of October.
TIME: The course record was set in 1994 by Gavin Bland in 3.02.49 (women's 1996 by Menna Angharad in 3.28.14). For mere mortals, expect somewhere around 4 ½ to 5 ½ hours depending on fitness.
START: Llanberis Community Centre (GR 582599). Park in Llanberis but be aware of parking times and resrictions.
O.S MAP: 1:25,000 Sheet North Wales OL17.
GRADIENT: Very sustained, steep, ascents and descents throughout the whole of this route.
ACCESS: The route is mainly over common access land and National Park footpaths. However, the initial sections through Dinorwig Slate Quarries are privately owned by the hydro-electric generating company, "First Hydro". As landowners, they have a responsibility to stop people going anywhere other than the designated, official footpath/track through the quarry. There have been access issues with rock climbers in recent years but none to speak of with runners or walkers using the quarry tracks. However, please try to keep a low profile and be vigilant regarding any security patrols. Please avoid confrontation if challenged but, add you are aware of the risks and dangers involved and then… run like hell!!

Grid References

582601	Gilfach Ddu Slate Museum
594605	Dinorwig Slate Quarries
600615	Top of the slate quarries
613613	Summit of Elidir Fawr 924m.
630595	Y Garn
636585	Llyn y Cŵm
643579	Glyder Fawr
640567	'Spot height' 646m
647556	Pen-y-Pass Youth Hostel
635545	Llyn Llydaw Reservoir
599537	'Watkin Path'
610544	Snowdon summit
608549	Junction of footpaths
587654	Moel Cynghorion (647m)
578573	Maesgwm
576584	Footpath next to Afon Arddu stream
579589	Snowdon Mountain Railway tracks

FGS Grading: Grading is F13 [D2, N3, T2, R3, H3]

Distance	**2**	12 – 18 miles.
Navigation	**3**	Expert navigation skills needed.
Terrain	**2**	25 – 50% on graded track or path 50 -75% off track.
Remoteness	**3**	Remote, isolated location.
Height	**3**	Over 250 ft per mile.

Stop press. As this book was going to print the height of Glyder Fawr has been upgraded from 999 metres to 1,000.8 metres. As it will take a couple of years for the OS to update their maps it has been decided to leave all references to this mountain as they were in order to correspond to the OS map.

Route Description :

1. Starting at the Llanberis Community Centre, run along the road to the slate museum, Gilfach Ddu (**GR 582601**). Continue towards Vivian Quarry Diving Centre.Turn sharp right here and ascend the old quarry 'incline'. Remain on this as it enters the main area of the disused Dinorwig Slate Quarries at **GR 594605**.

2. Turn left here, passing a huge derelict quarry building on your right. Immediately after this you will arrive at a gate saying, "Private Road. No public Access". Keeping a 'low-profile', climb over this gate(!) and follow the zig-zag quarry road as it wends its way from level to level. The quarry scenery is spectacular in its own way and a stark reminder of the harshness of working in this environment over a hundred years ago.

At **GR 600615** the top of the quarries is reached. Continue straight upwards on a vague path due east taking the steep grass/ heather slope to the top of Elidir Fach (795m.). At its flat top, continue heading east until an uphill path is reached which rises diagonally and emerges on the rocky summit of Elidir Fawr (**GR 612613**). The path now descends over rocky blocks and boulders to a broken path marked as Bwlch y Marchlyn and Bwlch y Brecan on the OS map. Continue along this passing Foel Goch at 831m and on to Y Garn at 947m (**GR 630595**). At Y Garn, follow the defined, descending path to Llyn y Cŵm (**GR 636585**). Follow this track until it converges with a more defined, rocky path that leads steeply upwards to Glyder Fawr at 999m.(**GR 643579**). At the top of Glyder Fawr, the route becomes less defined with no real marked path to follow. Take a line that more or less descends the blunt spur off Glyder Fawr in a southerly direction towards the Llanberis Pass and 'spot height' 646m (**GR 640567**) on a compass bearing of 186 degrees south. Here, descend south easterly towards Pen-y-Pass Youth Hostel at **GR 647556**, bearing 145 degrees.

3. At Pen-y-Pass you will be able to replenish liquid supplies and use the toilet or café facilities (if required) and decide whether to continue the

View of the route from Elidir Fawr looking South East towards Y Garn and Glyder Fawr in the far distance. Photo by Julia Kelly.

run or 'bail out' here and wait for the bus back to Llanberis! Hopefully, the latter option will be ignored and one will continue to run. However, bear in mind that the most arduous section is still ahead of you. From PYP, run along the Miner's Track as far as Llyn Llydaw Reservoir (**GR 635545**). Deviate here onto the path that leads steeply up the eastern flanks of Lliwedd, scrambling up some easy rock sections as it wends its way to the East Peak of Lliwedd at 893m and on to the slightly higher West Peak at 898m. A steep descent over boulders and scree eventually converges with the 'Watkin Path' at **GR 599537**. Here the route flattens somewhat. However, this respite is shortly lived as one approaches the very steep and loose path that leads up to the summit of Snowdon itself at 1085m (**GR 610544**). During May to October the new Snowdon café is open for drinks and snacks etc. if required. It is fair to say, at this point, you will be quite fatigued and it is essential to maintain your body's hydration. You still have one or two big hurdles ahead of you.

4. Descend off Snowdon to **GR 608549**, where several paths meet. Take the path which descends north westerly above Clogwyn Du'r Arddu and marked on the map as the 'Snowdon Ranger Footpath'. Run along this for some distance until a fence is reached at the base of Moel Cynghorion (647m), (**GR 587654**). Run, walk or 'crawl' the unrelenting grassy slope to its top, possibly pondering why you were daft enough to choose this run in the first place!

5. At the top of Moel Cynghorion the end is, thankfully, in sight. A long, steep, wet, boggy descent in a north westerly direction over grass, tussocks and reeds (joy!) leads down into the valley known as Maesgwm (**GR 578573**). Locate a convenient point at which to ford the stream and climb up to reach the well defined path that leads to Llanberis. At **GR 576584** take a right turn and follow a narrower path that runs next to the Afon Arddu stream and crosses the tracks of the Snowdon Mountain Railway at **GR 579589** (see photo set). Continue running downwards taking the path beside 'Pen y Ceunant' tea rooms as it descends through the woods of Coed Victoria. This emerges at a stile opposite the Royal Victoria Hotel. Now turn left and run, limp or hobble through Llanberis village, finding 'sanctuary' at Pete's Eats. Congratulations. With 8,500 ft. of ascent behind you, you have just bagged one of the best long-distance mountain runs in Snowdonia. A pint of Pete's tea never tasted so good!

Competitors in the final stage of Peris Horseshoe 2010 event crossing the Snowdon Mountain Railway before the descent into Llanberis via Coed Victoria

CNICHT
ROUTE 20

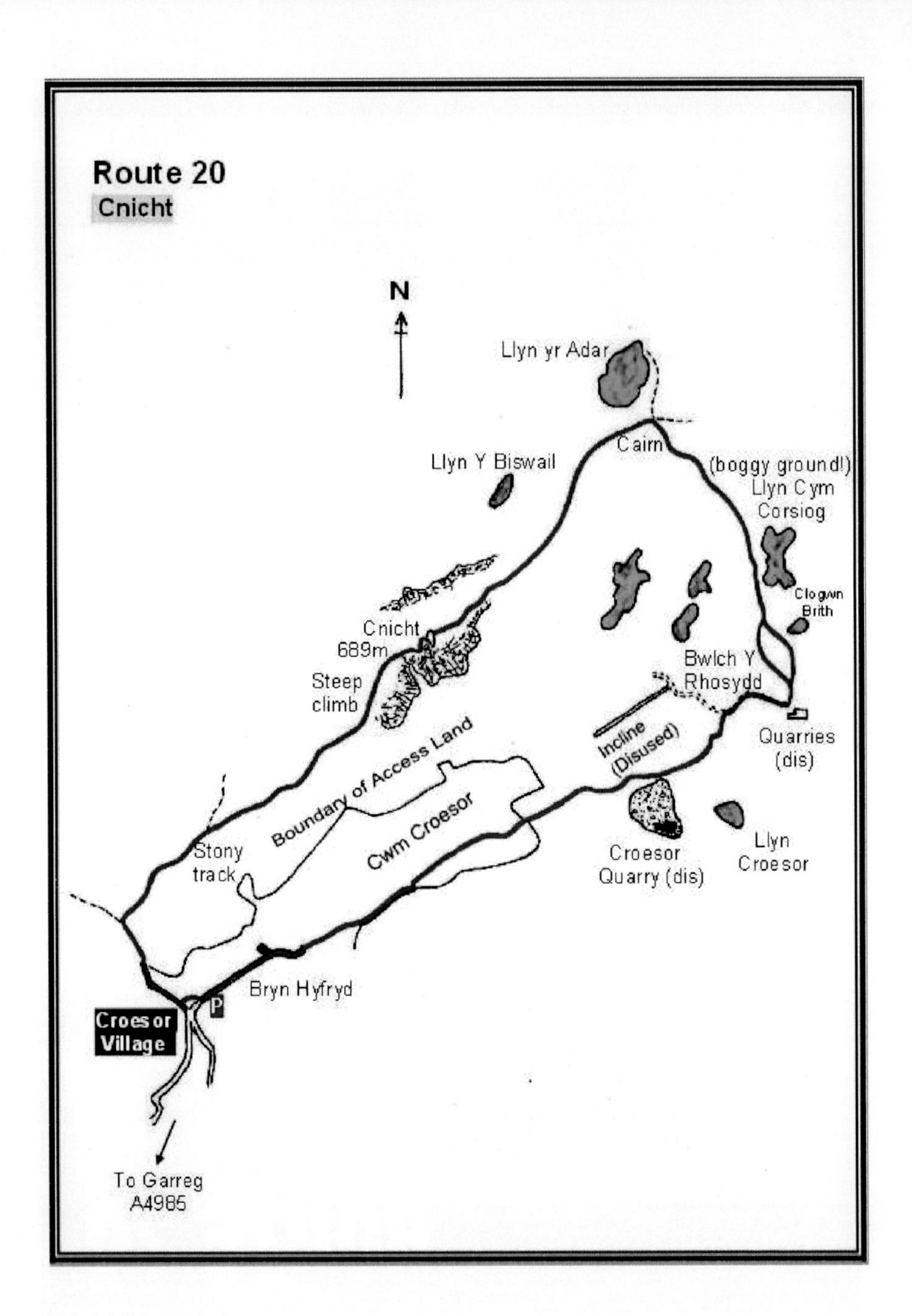
Route 20
Cnicht
N
Llyn yr Adar
Cairn
Llyn Y Biswail
(boggy ground!)
Llyn Cym
Corsiog
Clogwn
Brith
Cnicht
689m
Steep
climb
Bwlch Y
Rhosydd
Quarries
(dis)
Boundary of Access Land
Incline
(Disused)
Cwm Croesor
Stony
track
Croesor
Quarry (dis)
Llyn
Croesor
Bryn Hyfryd
P
Croesor
Village
To Garreg
A4985

ROUTE 20: CNICHT

DISTANCE: 6 Miles
ASCENT: Min.165 metres @ start. Max. 689 metres.
TERRAIN: The effects of glaciation between 26,000 and 11,000 years ago can be seen clearly in this delightful mountain and valley run. Nicknamed the 'Welsh Matterhorn', Cnicht shows the effects of what is called 'back to back glacial erosion', so common in the Alps. It has to be a contender for the 'best looking' mountain in North Wales! The initial half of this run uses a steep rocky pathway with some steep scrambling sections on the upper approach slopes to the summit. From here a peat moorland path is followed across short grass which becomes boggy (*very* boggy in Autumn and Winter!) in the latter section. A narrow return path descends all the way to Croesor Village with one or two slippery bits where hillside springs emerge. In misty conditions, navigation and route finding between GR's 657477 and 663463 can be tricky due to the nature of marshland and lakes in this area. Some of the paths are very much undefined.
TIME: 1hour 30 – 40 minutes.
START: Croesor Village car park (GR 631447) marked on map as 'Bryn-y-Gelynen'. Free car park with toilet facility.
O.S MAP: 1:25,000 Sheet North Wales OL17.
GRADIENT: Sustained, steep, rocky climb to the summit of Cnicht with long, gentle descent to Croesor Village.
ACCESS: The run is on open country access land using defined and undefined pathways and tracks.

Grid References

631447	Croesor Village free car park.
621451	Right turn through gate towards Cnicht.
645466	Summit of Cnicht.
655480	Llyn yr Adar.
657477	Path junction and cairn.
665466	Llyn Clogwyn Brith.
663463	Bwlch y Rhosydd quarry track.

FGS Grading: Grading is: F8 [D1, N2, T1, R1, H3]

Distance	**1**	6 – 12 miles.
Navigation	**2**	Competent navigation skills needed.
Terrain	**1**	50 – 75% on graded track or path 25 -50% off track.
Remoteness	**1**	Countryside in fairly close proximity to habitation – at least 80% of the route within 2 miles.
Height	**3**	Over 250 ft per mile.

The author, Jim Kelly, running the quarry track section at 'Bwlch-y-Rhossydd. Photo by Julia Kelly.

Route Description :

1. From the car park entrance, turn right and run for a short distance on the village road as it ascends the hillside. This turns into a farm track after a few hundred yards. At **GR 621451** take a right turn through a gate on to open country, following a rough, stony path. Stay on this to **GR 634455** where the path splits. Take the less-defined right hand branch which follows a blunt ridge upwards towards the 318m spot height, in a north easterly direction. Remain on this path as it rises steeply towards the triangular mass of Cnicht, getting more rocky as one progresses.

The rocky summit triangle of Cnicht showing the ascent path right of the steep grey cliffs in the centre of the photo. Photo by Julia Kelly.

Some of the rocky steps are quite worn and 'polished' so take care with your footing here. After a bit of a 'leg-pump' you will arrive at the rocky summit of Cnicht at 689m. The views from here, on a clear day, are simply superb. The whole panorama of Snowdonia can be seen before you.

2. Now continue to run north easterly on a grassy moorland path that descends to a flat area near Llyn yr Adar at **GR 655480** (great views of Snowdon here!). At **GR 657477** you arrive at a path junction (cairn marking the spot). Run in a south easterly direction as the path descends over rocks and marshy ground towards Cwn Corsiog (553m) and Llyn Cwn Corsiog. Take care here as the route becomes quite undefined and can be quite boggy underfoot even in dry weather. In Autumn and Winter expect to get a thorough soaking! Your next landmark is Llyn Clogwyn Brith (**GR 665466**). Now run south for a short distance ending up at some old disused slate quarry buildings and a defined quarry road, marked as Bwlch-y-Rhosydd (**GR 663463**) on the map.

3. Run along this track as it becomes 'elevated'. As it curves round locate a leftward descending path that crosses a small stream. This path now descends gently all the way down the valley towards Croesor Village passing Moelwyn Bank at **GR 641453**. A tarmac road is now followed for half a mile or so until one arrives back at the village car park.

LLYN PADARN
ROUTE 21

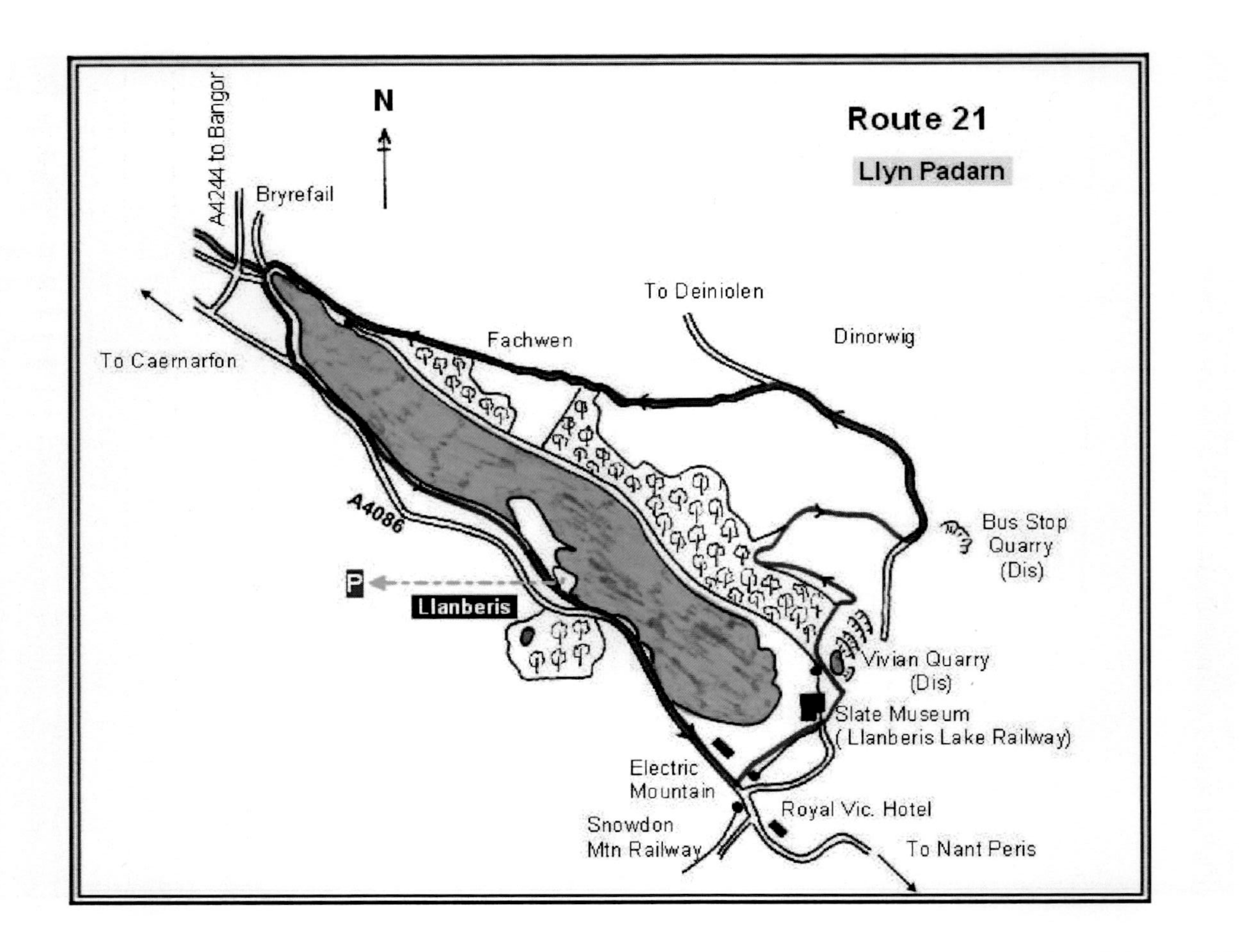
Route 21
Llyn Padarn
N
A4244 to Bangor
Bryrefail
To Caernarfon
Fachwen
To Deiniolen
Dinorwig
A4086
P
Llanberis
Bus Stop
Quarry
(Dis)
Vivian Quarry
(Dis)
Slate Museum
(Llanberis Lake Railway)
Electric
Mountain
Royal Vic. Hotel
Snowdon
Mtn Railway
To Nant Peris

ROUTE 21: LLYN PADARN

DISTANCE: 6.25 Miles
ASCENT: Min.109 metres @ start. Max.300 metres.
TERRAIN: Although 'technically' just outside the Snowdonia National Park boundary, this route has been included as it serves as a great little run when inclement weather prevents one from running on the high fells and mountains. The majority of this hill run is on good paths, tracks and roads. Off-road fell shoes are not necessary; a good pair of road shoes will suffice. The route is surprisingly steep as it climbs the series of slate steps through the quarry section, Do not underestimate it!
TIME: 55 Mins - 1 Hr 05M
START: Padarn Country Park car park GR 574609
O.S MAP: 1:25,000 Sheet North Wales OL17.
GRADIENT: Generally easy or flat. One steep, continuous section through the slate quarries.
ACCESS: No access issues. Sections of this run are on land owned by Padarn Country Park. Please stay on the paths and tracks.

Grid References

574609	Padarn Country Park lakeside car park.
585603	Slate Museum – 'Gilfach Ddu'
585609	Narrow, downhill path
591611	Bus turn-around at Dinorwig Quarry.
584618	Left turn into minor road towards Fachwen.
572619	Fachwen Village.
563618	'Hole in the wall' to disused railway line.

FGS Grading: Grading is F4 [D0, N1, T0, R1, H3]

Distance	**0**	Up to 6 miles
Navigation	**1**	Basic navigation skills needed
Terrain	**0**	75% + on graded track or path
Remoteness	**1**	Countryside in fairly close proximity to habitation – at least 80% of the route within 2 miles
Height	**2**	Over 125 ft per mile

Route Description :

1. From the car park turn left and run along the tarmac road to the A4086. Continue along this for a short distance until a path leads one down towards the edge of Llyn Padarn and past the children's play park. Run along the lakeside as the path crosses a grassy field ending up at the bridge over the 'outflow' between Llyn Peris Reservoir and Llyn Padarn. Turn left after the bridge and, before the slate museum ('Gilfach Ddu' **GR 585603**), cross the road taking a gently rising access road that passes the climbing and diving area of 'Vivian Quarry'.

Approaching the steep stepped section at the side of Vivian Quarry.
Photo by Julia Kelly.

After a short distance the path turns a sharp right and continues upwards through the woods. Locate the steep slate steps (marked by a country park blue marker post). Remain on these as they weave their way up the hillside, keeping Vivian Quarry to your right.

Photo by Julia Kelly.

2. At the top of the steps locate a rough track and run north westerly past trees to your right. At **GR 585609** continue running downhill on a narrow path that swings round to the right through trees until another track is reached. Follow this steadily uphill towards Dinorwig Slate Quarries and the bus turn-around point (**GR 591611**).

3. At the gate, turn left and run on the road in the direction of Dinorwig Village. At GR 584618 turn left and follow the minor road as it twists and descends to 'Fachwen' (**GR 572619**). Shortly after, you will arrive at the head of Llyn Padarn with its spectacular view south east up the valley and towards the Llanberis Pass. Real picture postcard stuff.. as they say! Cross the road bridge and trend left, climbing a ladder stile which places you on the 'old defunct Llanberis road', now used as a tarmac field and 'latrine' for cows… nice! Crossing another ladder stile, run along the A4086 pavement for a short distance until a 'hole in the wall' (**GR 563618**) on the left allows one to descend onto an old former railway line, now used as a public footpath. Run This for approximately ¾'s of a mile until you arrive at the tarmac road that leads you back to Llyn Padarn car park.

ROUTE 22
LLYN DINAS / ABERGLASYN / BEDDGELERT / INTEGRALE

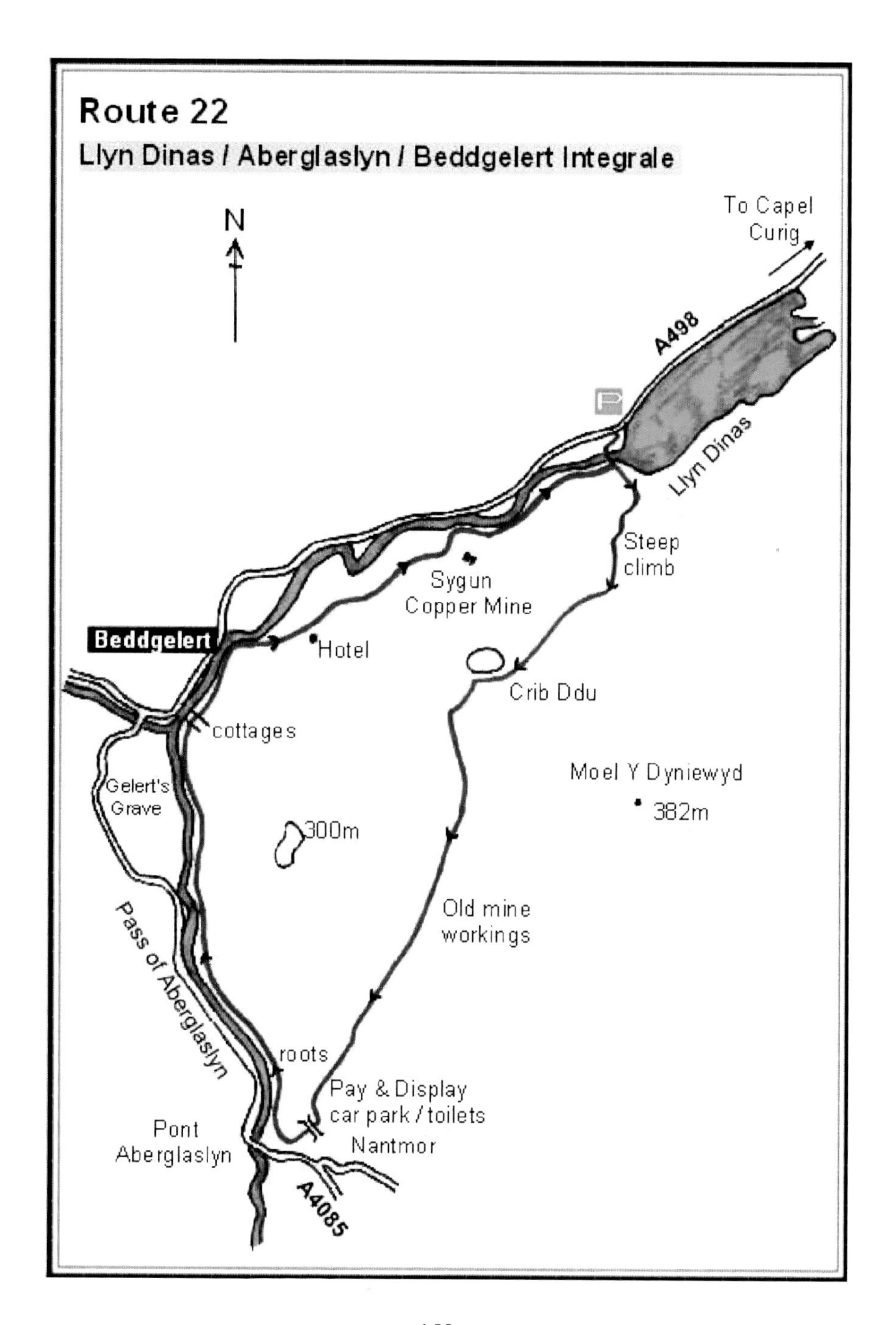
Route 22
Llyn Dinas / Aberglaslyn / Beddgelert Integrale
N
To Capel Curig
A498
Llyn Dinas
Steep climb
Sygun Copper Mine
Beddgelert
Hotel
Crib Ddu
cottages
Moel Y Dyniewyd
382m
Gelert's Grave
300m
Old mine workings
Pass of Aberglaslyn
roots
Pay & Display car park / toilets
Pont Aberglaslyn
Nantmor
A4085

ROUTE 22:
LLYN DINAS / ABERGLASYN / BEDDGELERT INTER-GALE

DISTANCE: 5.5 Miles
ASCENT: Min. 53 metres @ start. Max. 300 metres.
TERRAIN: This route is entirely on defined footpaths, tracks and minor roads. However, some sections are quite narrow and rocky and can become muddy and slippery in the wet. Care needed on the Aberglaslyn footpath.
TIME: 1 Hr 20 Mins
START: At the lay-by just south west of Llyn Dinas on the A498.
O.S MAP: 1:25,000 Sheet North Wales OL17.
GRADIENT: One short steep section at the beginning of the run. Thereafter, reasonably angled and mainly downhill or on the flat.
ACCESS: The majority of this run is on open country access land with some sections on public minor roads.

Grid References

609504	Parking at Llyn Dinas
613477	Moel y Dyniewyd
612487	Top of steep path.
597463	Pont Glaslyn
606487	Sygyn Copper Mine.

FGS Grading: Grading is F8 [D1, N1,T1, R2, H3]

Distance	**1**	6 – 12 miles
Navigation	**1**	Basic navigation skills needed
Terrain	**1**	50 – 75% on graded track or path 25 -50% off track
Remoteness	**2**	Countryside not in close proximity to habitation – less than 20% of the route within 2 miles
Height	**3**	Over 250 ft per mile

Route Description :

1. Park in the lay-by just beyond the southern end of Llyn Dinas, **GR 609494**. Run back up towards the lake, locating a footpath that takes you through some trees to a footbridge that crosses the lake outflow. Continue gently upwards taking the track that climbs the mountainside towards Moel y Dyniewyd **GR 613477**. This gradually steepens as it weaves its way to the top. At **GR 612487** it flattens out as it heads south west towards Grib Ddu. Great views of the Snowdon group of mountains north of here. After a short distance, the path rises once again as it tops out at Bwlch y Sygyn (318m). Here a stile is met. Climb over this and begin the long, delightful, grassy descent towards Aberglaslyn, passing some interesting industrial relics dating back to the bygone age of copper mining in the area.

Ryley Redhead descending past the disused copper mines on the long descent towards Aberglaslyn. Photo by Julia Kelly.

2. Eventually, after passing under a railway bridge, you will arrive at a car park and toilets. This is Pont Glaslyn, **GR 597463**. Now run up a narrow track through the trees (exposed roots. care!) which, after a couple of hundred metres, drops down to Pont Glaslyn and the picturesque, Aberglaslyn River Gorge. The narrow path weaves its way through trees high above the river which is now below you. Its probable that you will encounter walkers along here. Please give way to them on the narrow sections. Continue over rocks until the path broadens out. The terrain from here is relatively flat and 'fast' all the way into Beddgelert and beyond.

3. Run past some delightful cottages staying on a well defined track through Rhododendron bushes. This eventually merges with a tarmac minor road that takes one past Sygyn Copper Mine tourist attraction, **GR 606487**. Follow the 'lakeside track' towards Llyn Dinas emerging at the wooden footbridge you crossed early on at the start of the route. Run back over the bridge and your car is less than a minute away!

LLANBERIS / ELIDIR FAWR / FOEL GOCH CIRCUIT
ROUTE 23

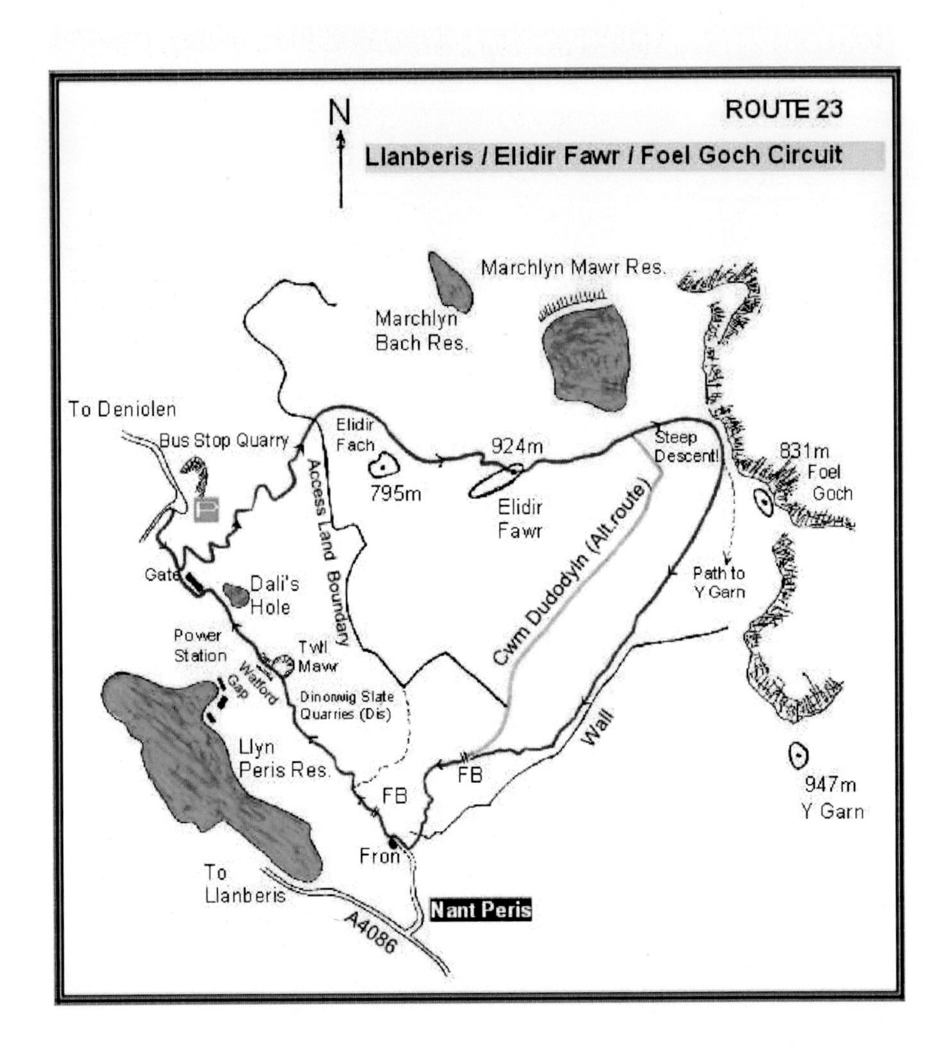

N
ROUTE 23
Llanberis / Elidir Fawr / Foel Goch Circuit
Marchlyn Mawr Res.
Marchlyn
Bach Res.
To Deniolen
Bus Stop Quarry
Elidir
Fach
795m
924m
Elidir
Fawr
Steep
Descent!
831m
Foel
Goch
Access Land Boundary
Cwm Dudodyln (Alt.route)
Path to
Y Garn
Gate
Dali's
Hole
Power
Station
Twll
Mawr
Watford
Gap
Dinorwig Slate
Quarries (Dis)
Wall
Llyn
Peris Res.
FB
FB
947m
Y Garn
Fron
To
Llanberis
Nant Peris
A4086

ROUTE 23: LLANBERIS / EIDER FAWR / FOEL GOCH CIRCUIT

DISTANCE: 7 Miles
ASCENT: Min. 300 metres @ start. Max. 924 metres.
TERRAIN: Elidir Fawr rises majestically above the northern side of Llanberis watching over the immense, surreal landscape that forms the famous Dinorwic Slate Quarries. These quarries have been the backdrop for many T.V. and film scenes, notably, the 2009 Hollywood remake of *"Clash of the Titans."* This circular route includes some dramatic, exposed, high terrain for the mountain runner, over a variety of rock types and surfaces. The lower stages of Foel Goch can become rather soggy after heavy rain so be prepared for wet feet! The 'setting' is superb and has a remote, 'high mountain feel' to it. A hydration pack containing fluid, windproofs, map & compass and whistle etc. is advisable. This route also forms the initial stages of the much longer and much more more arduous, Peris Horseshoe Circuit (see previous Route 19).
TIME: 1¾ – 2 hrs allowing for navigation stops etc.
START: 'Bus Stop Quarry' parking area, Dinorwig.
O.S MAP: 1:25,000 Sheet North Wales OL17.
GRADIENT: Continually steep ascents through the slate quarries, and on to Elidir Fach and Elidir Fawr. Pleasant, fast, grassy downhill sections thereafter.
ACCESS: DinorwIc Slate Quarries are owned and managed by the electricity generating company, First Hydro Ltd. Whilst they are supportive of local running events, they have a 'duty of care' to erect signs to warn the 'general public' about the dangers of venturing up in to the disused quarries. Apart from issues concerning rock climbers over the years, no confrontations are known between First Hydro's security personnel and fell runners using the site. However, if challenged, please explain you are aware of and accept the risks and continue your run. No known access issues exist for the remainder of this route.

Grid References

591611	Parking area and start of the run.
598614	Top of the slate quarries.
600616	Hairpin bend in the road.
604613	Elidir Fach.
612613	Elidir Fawr.
617620	Marchlyn Mawr Reservoir
620615	Descent to Cwm Dudodyn
628612	Foel Goch

625616 Narrow, eroded path
605590 'Fron'
598598 'Victoria'

FGS Grading: Grading is: F11 [D1, N2, T2, R3, H3]

Distance	**1**	6 – 12 miles
Navigation	**2**	Competent navigation skills needed.
Terrain	**2**	25 – 50% on graded track or path. 50 – 75% off track.
Remoteness	**3**	Remote isolated location.
Height	**3**	Over 250 ft per mile

The Author, Jim Kelly approaching the summit rocks on Elidir Fawr at 924m.
Photo by Julia Kelly.

Route Description :

1. Begin this run at the parking/ turn-around area known as "Bus Stop Quarry", situated at the termination of the Deiniolen/ Dinorwig road (**GR 591611**). Run through the obvious metal kissing gate that allows access to the pedestrian 'right of way' through the disused slate quarries, via the old quarry road.

Negotiating the winding quarry track in the impressive Dinorwic Slate Quarries. Photo by Julia Kelly.

After a short distance, a metal gate on the left is met (before a huge derelict building) with a sign saying "Private Road. No public Access". Climb over this gate and follow the zig-zag quarry track up through the many 'levels' to the top of the hill (see Access notes for this section of the run).

2. At **GR 598614**, the top of the slate quarries are reached. A broken stile by a metal gate allows access to a surfaced minor road which makes its way gently uphill and then hairpins sharp right. At the hairpin (**GR 600616**), clamber up the steep bank and begin the long ascent, in an easterly direction, towards the top of Elidir Fach (compass bearing from the hairpin: 114 degrees). The running surface here requires you to negotiate heather, tussocks and surface rocks. Watch your footing! After approximately 0.6 km, you will arrive at a flat grassy area with Elidir Fach (795m) to your right (**GR 604613**).

3.Elidir Fawr still rises a considerable way ahead of you. Now locate the narrow, stony path that rises diagonally to the rocky summit of Elidir Fawr (924m) at **GR 612613**. On a clear day, the 360 degree view of

The Rocky North Western slope of Elidir Fawr viewed from Elidir Fach. The narrow, stony path to the summit can clearly be seen in the centre of the picture. Photo by Julia Kelly.

Northern Snowdonia from the summit is exceptional!

4. At this point, carefully descend almost due East (85 degrees) over rocks and boulders, eventually connecting with a narrow, broken path that runs around the rocky rim, high above Marchlyn Mawr Reservoir (**GR 617620**). This is the 'water feed' to the hydro-electric power station that lies hundreds of feet beneath you inside the 'Electric Mountain!' At **GR 620615** there is a steep and unstable (and not at all pleasant!) 'alternative' descent route that takes one through the wet and boggy, Cwm Dudodyn. Apart from it being shorter, from past experience, I cannot think of one reason why anyone would opt to use this! Best left to the "connoisseur of the grim and unpleasant!" Its inclusion here is for completeness only.

Running along the narrow broken path at Bwlch y Brecan. Photo by Julia Kelly.

5. So, ignoring the alternative route, continue to run around the top of the cwm, marked as 'Bwlch y Brecan' and on towards Foel Goch (831m) at **GR 628612**. Remain on this path as it runs almost parallel to the 710m contour line, leading in a southerly direction. At **GR 625616**, a narrow, eroded path is reached, branching off right and gently descending the hill slope in a south westerly direction for approximately 2.4 kms. ***(Note. This is not marked on the OS Map and should not be confused with the public footpath descending south west from Bwlch y Cywion to Nant Peris!)***

6. It passes over 2 ladder stiles in its lower half and can get quite 'soggy' after heavy rain. Nevertheless, this is a very pleasant descent which joins the final section of the aforementioned 'Alternative Route' at a small footbridge and gate. Continue to run downhill over uneven farmland and rough grazing to another ladder stile over a wall next to a holly tree. Continue descending (often muddy!!) to emerge on a tarmac farm road leading to the dwelling marked on the map as 'Fron' (**GR 605590**). Run towards Fron, passing in front of the house and up to a stile. The path continues over rough grazing land and rocks to a small footbridge over a stream. This leads down a grassy path towards and over another footbridge and a metal gate. Here the path rises again and follows a narrow quarry workers' 'stepped' track which emerges onto a larger quarry road that leads uphill to 'Victoria' (**GR 598598**). Remain on this road, passing Twll Mawr (The Big Hole), and through the point known as 'Watford Gap' and on to the, now fenced off (for safety reasons!), Dali's Hole Lake.

7. The road now rises gently, passing through a metal kissing gate with the huge derelict quarry building now on your right hand side. The gate you initially climbed over is a short way ahead! From here you are less than a few minutes from your car with the time to reflect on what has been one of the area's classic mountain runs.

ABER TO FOEL FRAS CIRCUIT
ROUTE 24

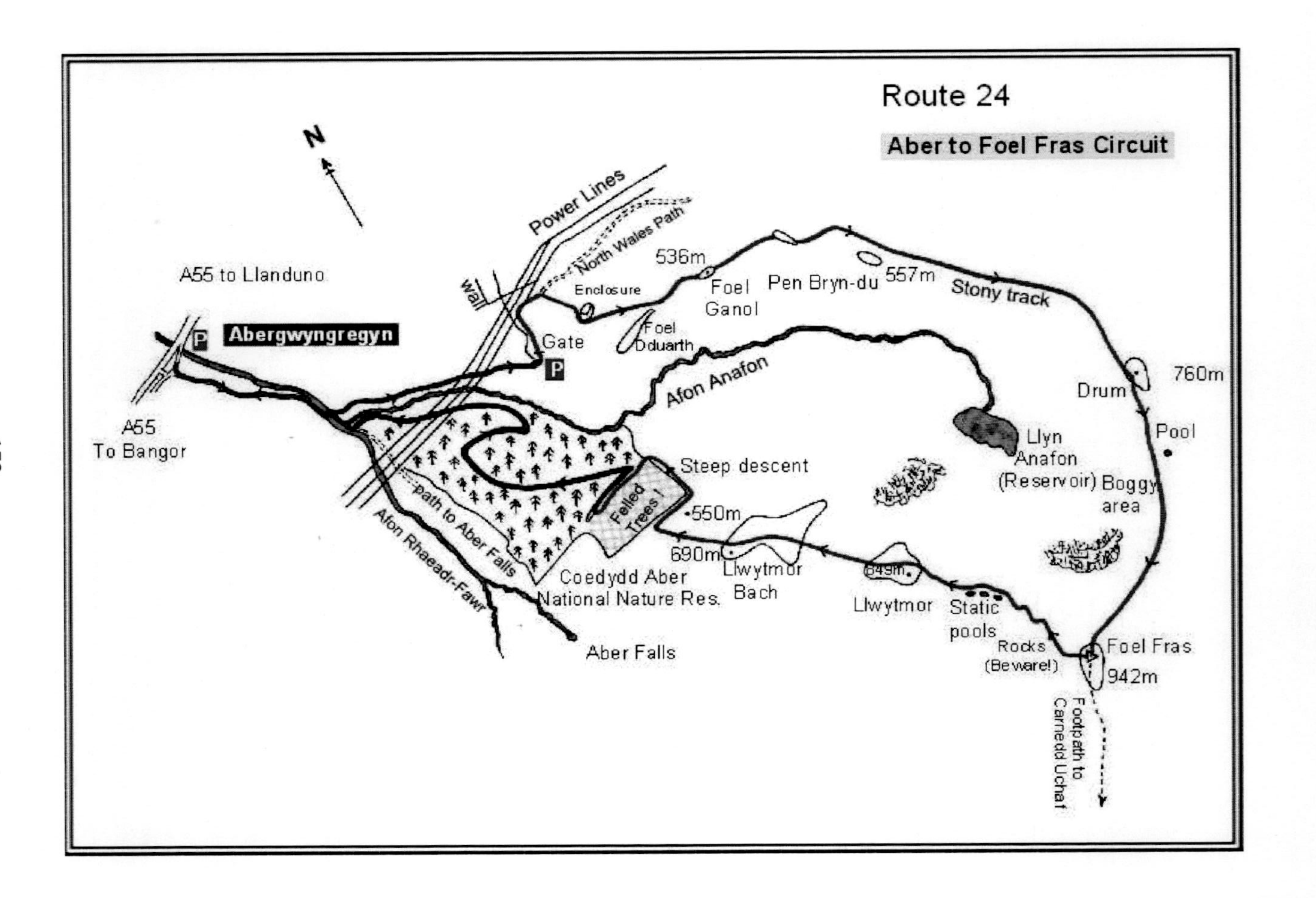

Route 24
Aber to Foel Fras Circuit
N
Power Lines
North Wales Path
536m
A55 to Llandudno
wall
Enclosure
Foel
Ganol
Pen Bryn-du
557m
Stony track
P
Abergwyngregyn
Foel
Dduarth
Gate
P
Afon Anafon
760m
Drum
A55
To Bangor
Pool
Llyn
Anafon
(Reservoir)
Boggy
area
Steep descent
Felled
Trees !
•550m
path to Aber Falls
Afon Rhaeadr-Fawr
690m
Llwytmor
Bach
849m
Coedydd Aber
National Nature Res.
Llwytmor
Static
pools
Rocks
(Beware!)
Foel Fras
942m
Aber Falls
Footpath to
Carnedd Uchaf

ROUTE 24: ABER TO FOEL FRAS CIRCUIT

DISTANCE: 11 Miles
ASCENT: Min. 30 metres @ start. Max. 942 metres.
TERRAIN: This circular route is a bit of a fell running 'cocktail!' Over its 11 mile distance, just about all elements of terrain are encountered; road, track, steep, grassy ascents/descents, boggy areas, rocks & boulders and a forestry trail. All this is set within a beautiful, remote location which forms the early stages of a traverse of the Carneddau Peaks from Aber to the Ogwen Valley. However, it is an open, exposed route over high ground which is susceptible to sudden changes in weather conditions. It should not be underestimated. As a result, it is vital that a map and compass are carried along with bad weather running kit. The early stage of this run follows that of Route 1; Aber Falls. Also, take care on the rocky boulder sections. The rocks can become quite slippery during damp or wet weather. Not the place to turn an ankle!
TIME: 2 ½ - 3 hours depending on ground conditions, weather and stops.
START: Abergwyngregyn Village free parking area by recyling centre.
O.S MAP: 1:25,000 Sheet North Wales OL17.
GRADIENT: Steep in places, sustained long ascents and descents throughout.
ACCESS: This is run almost entirely on open country access land. No known access issues.

Grid References

GR 676717	Free car parking area.
GR 688716	Foel Ganol 536m.
GR 694716	Yr Orsedd 559m.
GR 697712	Pen Bryn du 557m
GR 697682	Foel Fras summit 942m.
GR 689693	Llwytmor 849m.
GR 679704	South eastern corner of forestry plantation.

FGS Grading: Grading is F12 [D1, N3, T2, R3, H3]

Distance	**1**	6 – 12 miles
Navigation	**3**	Expert navigation skills needed.
Terrain	**2**	25 - 50% on graded track or path 50 – 75% off track.
Remoteness	**3**	Remote isolated location.
Height	**3**	Over 250 ft per mile

The author, Jim Kelly approaching the rocky summit of Foel Ganol 536 metres.
Photo Julia Kelly.

Route Description :

1. From the free car parking lay-by (a short distance up from the bus stop and turn-around point/recycling centre), run through Aber village passing the café, Hen Felin. Continue up the minor tarmac road until you arrive at the pay & display car park for Aber Falls. Cross the narrow road bridge over the Afon Rhaeadr Fawr and, instead of turning right up to the falls (see Route 1), run straight on and follow the gently rising road that is designated 'North Wales Path', until you reach another free parking area at **GR 676717**. Go through a gate and run up leftwards following a track beside a wall. After a short distance this swings around to the right. This is where you leave the 'N.W.P' and begin the steep climb up Foel Ganol (536m) at **GR 688716**. Begin by running across grassland, passing the area marked *"enclosure"* on the OS Map and locate a narrow path/sheep track that ascends the hillside to the rocky top of Foel Ganol. Proceed along the blunt ridge, passing Yr Orsedd (559m) at **GR 694716** and on to Pen Bryn du (557m) at **GR 697712**.

2. From the top of Pen Bryn du descend a steep, short grass slope to join the good, stony path that ascends to the rounded summit of Drum (750m). This area is normally quite wet and boggy at most times of the year, especially in the autumn and winter months. So much so, that the National Park Authority have constructed stepping stones over the worst sections. However, it is highly likely that you will still get wet feet! Continue running uphill until you reach the trig point at the rocky Foel Fras summit (942m) at **GR 697682**.

3. From here, descend very carefully over angular rocks and boulders in a North Westerly direction towards Llwytmor (849m) at **GR 689693**. Yet again, this is often quite a wet and 'squelchy' section with no real defined path. In poor weather the compass bearing from Foel Fras to Llwytmor is 329 degrees. On reaching the rocky top of Llwytmor, continue running north westerly towards its neighbour, Llwytmor Bach. Similarly, there is no defined route here and the terrain consists of boulders and heather tussocks over steep, uneven ground. From

Approaching the top of Llwytmor 849 metres with Foel Fras just completed, in the distance.

Llwytmor Bach (690m) all the uphill sections are now over. Descend the steep, uneven grass slope of Llwytmor Bach's northern slope towards the south eastern corner of Coedydd Aber National Nature Reserve forestry plantation, at **GR 679704**.

4. Please note, although the map illustrates this as a 'green area', this whole southern section of the woodland has been extensively chopped and all that remains is a surreal, dense landscape of white, weathered tree stumps, roots and sharp branches. **Do not attempt to run through these!** Instead, follow a rough track that ends up at the top of a shallow, grassy gully. Descend this, following a broken wall until you are forced to turn left and follow a path alongside a wire fence. After a short distance, a stile/gate is met. Cross this and run down the wide, gravel forest road, passing the rusting remains of forestry machinery, all the way to the Aber Falls tourist path and the pay & display car park.

Approaching the pine woodland of Coedydd Aber National Nature Reserve from Llwytmor Bach, showing the extensive tree felling that has taken place in recent years.

5. Now retrace your strides down the tarmac road to Aber village and the sanctuary of the Hen Felin Café... if you have timed it right that is!

YR EIFL - MYNYDD CARNGUWCH CIRCUIT
ROUTE 25

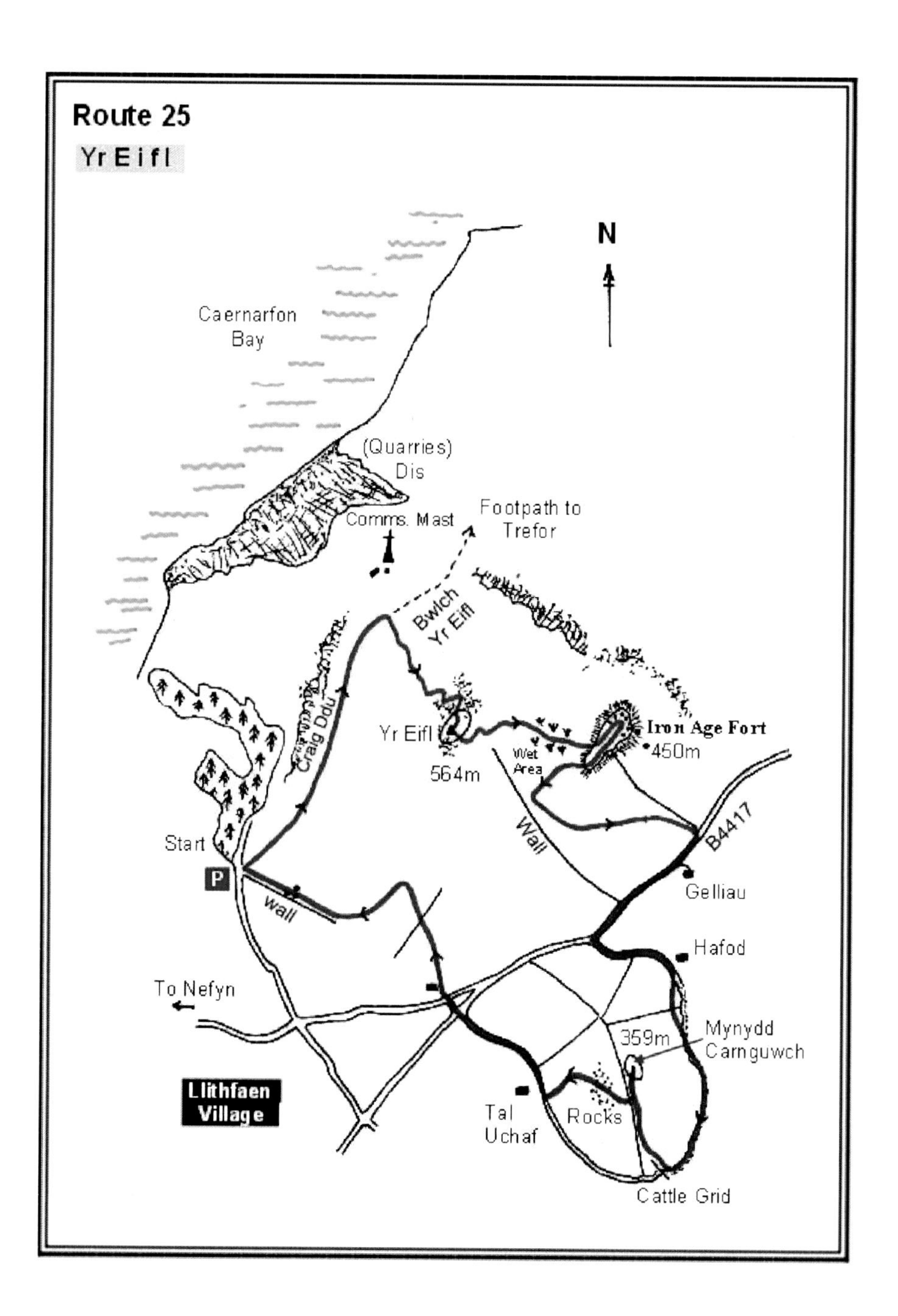

Route 25
Yr Eifl
N
Caernarfon Bay
(Quarries) Dis
Comms. Mast
Footpath to Trefor
Bwlch Yr Eifl
Craig Ddu
Yr Eifl
564m
Wet Area
Iron Age Fort
450m
Wall
B4417
Start
P
wall
Gelliau
Hafod
To Nefyn
359m
Mynydd Carnguwch
Llithfaen Village
Tal Uchaf
Rocks
Cattle Grid

ROUTE 25: YR EIFL – MYNYDD CARNGUWCH CIRCUIT

DISTANCE: 7 Miles (longer & shorter variations exist)
ASCENT: Min. 280 metres @ start. Max. 564 metres.
TERRAIN: The beautiful landscape around Yr Eifl remains one of North Wales' best kept secrets. Strangely, the paradox here is perhaps it is one of the most viewed series of mountains from car windows of people heading towards the boating resorts of Pwlhelli and Abersoch! As a result, you would think it would be inundated by tourists visiting the area. Not so!
For the mountain runner, it presents a largely man-made terrain that has been influenced by people since pre-Iron Age times. The 'centrepiece' of this evidence is the Iron-Age hill fort of Tre'r Ceiri (Bryngaer Oes yr Haearn), one of the biggest and best preserved forts of its type in the whole of Britain! This route runs straight through it! It scores highly on every twist and turn; good quality tracks and paths, fantastic mountain and coastal views, challenging gradients and a large variety of points of interest along the way. All this amounts to making it one of the best runs in this guide. Used in conjunction with the OS Map, there is also scope to either extend or reduce the distance of the route chosen here. It is an absolute 'gem'!
TIME: 2 – 2 ½ hours (depending on stops and, if exploring the Iron Age Fort!
START: Free (at time of writing!) car park above the village of Llithfaen, signposted towards the hill fort, 'Tre'r Ceiri.'
O.S MAP: 1:25,000 Sheet North Wales 254.
GRADIENT: Steep ascents of 'Yr Eifl' and 'Mynydd Carnguwch'.
ACCESS: No known access issues. However, at GR 365433 the route uses a public footpath that runs up someone's lovely driveway and around the back of their house to a gate, leading to open country! PLEASE CAUSE AS LITTLE DISTURBANCE AS POSSIBLE HERE!

Grid References

353441	Car park above village of Llithfaen.
362467	Communications mast & station.
366447	Summit of Yr Eifl.
375447	Iron Age hill fort.
377435	'Hafod'.
376424	Cattle grid
375429	Summit of Mynydd Carnguwch
369428	'Tal-uchaf'
363439	Llŷn Coastal Footpath
356438	Engraved, grey granite information plaques

FGS Grading: Grading is: F9 [D1, N2, T2, R1, H3]

Distance	**1**	6 – 12 miles
Navigation	**2**	Competent navigation skills needed.
Terrain	**2**	25 - 50% on graded track or path 50 – 75% off track.
Remoteness	**1**	Countryside in fairly close proximity to habitation – at least 80% of the route with 2 miles.
Height	**3**	Over 250 ft per mile

Jim Kelly approaching the summit of Yr Eifl. Photo by Julia Kelly.

Route Description :

1. Begin at the large car park by the coniferous woods at **GR 353441**. Locate the start of the broad, stony track that runs alongside a line of telegraph poles. Follow this steadily uphill towards the communications mast and out-buildings (**GR 362467**). On reaching the section marked as 'Bwlch Yr Eifl' on the map, turn right across the heather and follow the rough, narrow footpath steeply uphill towards the summit of Yr Eifl. A series of small cairns mark this in its upper stages. Take care here with the large rocks and boulders; many are quite loose! Facing north, this section can also become quite icy on cold winter mornings!

The top of Yr Eifl (564m./ GR 366447) is clearly marked by a trig point and one of the best constructed cairns/wind shelters you are ever likely to come across! On a clear, sunny day, the views stretching towards

Running down of Yr Eifl towards the Iron Age Hillfort in the distance.
Photo by Julia Kelly.

Caernarfon Bay in the north and towards the ancient hill fort in the east are simply 'stunning!"

2. Now descend to the small narrow track that runs south easterly through heather and rocks. Instead of continuing straight down by a wall (see OS Map), trend more to the left, where a deviation in the path allows you run in a more east-north-easterly direction.

This path eventually flattens at a boggy section. It is possible, using a bit of cunning, to keep one's feet relatively dry!. After this the path heads upwards once more to the outer and inner walls of the fort (information board located here explaining the history of the site).

As you run to the very top of the fort at 485 metres (**GR 375447**), you will pass numerous relics of ancient 'Roundhouses' where the inhabitants would have lived in around A.D.78.

The view of your next challenge, Mynydd Carnguwch, viewed from the descent path from the Hillfort.

3. With the 'history lesson' over(!), it's time to get on with it and exit the fort via its south west gate and follow the good stepped path as it swings down and round eastwards, eventually ending up through a gate and on to the B4417. Take care here as the road is quite narrow in places and the traffic moves at quite a pace.

4. At the road, turn right. Run for ½ mile or so to the turning on the left, marked 'Hafod' (**GR 377435**). Cross the steel cattle grid and continue down the tarmac farm track. After a short way this track splits. Take the inclined, grassy track to the right. This contours its way all around the base of Mynydd Carnguwch (*nick-named the 'Tit'.. for obvious reasons relating to its overall shape!*), passing a telecoms station and through two metal gates. At the second gate, the track becomes a tarmac road once again which is followed to the cattle grid at **GR 376424**.

Watch the sheep flee!!! Jim Kelly approaching the rocky summit of Mynydd Carnguwch. Photo by Julia Kelly.

5. It is now time to switch to 'uphill mode' once again! At the cattle grid, run steeply uphill on a broken, stony path next to the obvious drystone wall. This continues all the way to the summit of Mynydd Carnguwch at 359m.(**GR 375429**) The rocky summit is quite loose. Take care not to turn an ankle here!

6. From the top, retrace your steps back down 50m or so towards the wall. A 'hole' in the stone blocks allows easy access to the western slope. Run carefully down this through heather, tussocks and concealed surface rocks (joy!) until both the angle and terrain improve. A grassy field system leads one to the sanctuary of the tarmac road yet again, emerging at the dwelling marked as 'Tal-uchaf' on the map (**GR 369428**). It may be wise here to 'empty' your running shoes of any heather twigs or plant debris that may have infiltrated them during this descent!

7. Proceed along the lane until the T-junction with the B4417 is reached. Cross straight over and follow the Public Footpath that goes up 'someone's' tarmac driveway towards their bungalow! Yes, this instruction is correct! A metal gate at the rear of their house leads back onto open country (see Access notes).

The grassy path gently rises to a point where the Llŷn Coastal Footpath crosses it (**GR 363439**). Take a left here and run down towards an access road. For the last time, the path begins to rise gently up and over a pleasant rise alongside a wall. At the top of the rise, 3 large sculptured boulders, with engraved, grey granite information plaques, indicate the 3 main viewpoints (**GR 356438**). From here you can clearly see the car park no more than a few minutes away. To complete this route with an evening sunset across the Irish Sea is simply magnificent!

"Remember, the light in Wales comes here to die every night."
Quote: John Redhead. Rock climbing legend. Photo by Julia Kelly.

Please note, this route can also be started and finished in the village of Trefor (**GR square 3746**). This adds a further 2.5 miles (approx.) to the route with no change in FGS Grading. Other variations also exist.

ROUTE "TICK" LIST					
ROUTE NO.	√	Date / Time Achieved	Weather Conditions	Partner(s) / Group	Remarks
1					
2					
3					
4					
5					
6					
7					
8					
9					
10					
11					
12					

ROUTE "TICK" LIST

ROUTE NO.	√	Date / Time Achieved	Weather Conditions	Partner(s) / Group	Remarks
13					
14					
15					
16					
17					
18					
19					
20					
21					
22					
23					
24					
25					

Jim Kelly: Jim Kelly was born in London in 1963. He first entered outdoor sports whilst at school in the late 1970's and early 80's. Climbing became his main passion with early ascents of Alpine Peaks such as Mont Blanc and Monte Rosa/ Dufourspitze between 1982 and 1983. Thereafter, Jim went on to instruct climbing and caving at several outdoor centres in England and Wales. In 1988 he moved to Sheffield in order to undertake a degree in Sports and Recreation Management. It also allowed him plenty of time to climb in the Peak District! More recently, Jim moved to North Wales where mountain running has become a new 'obsession' with him. It also happens to be where he met Julia, his wife. In his first 18 months of running Jim has completed both the arduous Snowdonia Marathon (his first ever marathon attempt!) in 03:44:05 and went on to complete the International Snowdon Run in a very respectable 01:35:07. Although Jim now works in retailing, guide book writing and feature writing for running and climbing magazines is increasingly absorbing more and more of his spare time. With several other titles in the pipeline, the future looks set to become a whole lot busier for him!

Julia Kelly: Julia Kelly was born in Indonesia in 1967 where she trained as a merchandising manager for many big-name designer fashion houses. She came over to the UK in 2007 where she met and married Jim. Julia now works as a Product Manager for an International supplier of high-class linens and glass/ tableware to the "mega-yacht" industry. Julia has keen interests in rock climbing, mountain scrambling, photography and design. Her knowledge of information technology has been invaluable in the production of this guide.

Trailguides Limited and the Run Off-Road Series

Trailguides is a small independent publisher specialising in books for the outdoor enthusiast. Run Off-Road is the name adopted by Trailguides for it's publications aimed at the fell, hill, trail and mountain runner. This series of books is designed to promote the sport of off-road running in all it's many forms and to encourage the participants to improve and develop their abilities and skills in order to further increase their enjoyment of the sport.

Our range of coaching guides for the fell, trail and mountain runner have received acclaim and favourable reviews from all of the relevant UK governing bodies within the sport, the Fell Runners Association, the Scottish Hill Runners Association, the Trail Runners Association and the Welsh Fell Runners Association plus the Irish Mountain Runners Association. Written by qualified coaches who specialise in off-road running these books often receive comments that they are unique in their concept and, indeed, have even been called that in one issue of The Fellrunner magazine. Our guiding principle is that our books "don't just tell you what to do but they also tell you HOW to do it".

This concept has been recognised by sales not only in the UK but across the world. Books have been sold to Australia, Canada, El Salvador, Finland, France, Germany, Ireland, Italy, Netherlands, New Zealand, Norway, Slovakia, Slovenia, South Africa, Spain, Sweden, Switzerland and the US. The expertise and popularity of our books is judged by the number of runners who buy one and who then come back to purchase others within the series.

This is an evolving series of books that is constantly expanding and now with this publication, A Mountain Runner's Guide to Snowdonia, a new chapter is opened with the development of a series of guidebooks written specifically for the runner. Designed to both encourage runners to venture away from the dreaded tarmac and to also push their capabilities just a little bit, this series will develop into a range of guides that will cover the countryside throughout the country ranging from the mountain tops of Snowdonia to the rolling hills of the South Downs and the flat lands of Norfolk. This is a series of books that will appeal to all of the fell, mountain and trail runners out there.

See our website at www.trailguides.co.uk and subscribe to our newsletter for regular updates on our range of publications.

At the time of writing the titles in the series include:

An Introduction to Trail and Fell Running
Downhill Techniques for Off-Road Runners
Uphill Techniques for Off-road Runners
Terrain Training for Off-road Runners
Mountain Marathon Preparation
Navigation for Off-Road Runners
Long and Ultra Distance Off-Road Running

Coming soon
The Mountain Marathon Book